CORPORATE FINANCE
Passnotes

PEARSON

We work with leading authors to develop the strongest
educational materials in Finance, bringing cutting-edge
thinking and best learning practice to a global market.

Under a range of well-known imprints, including
Financial Times Prentice Hall, we craft high quality
print and electronic publications which help readers
to understand and apply their content, whether studying
or at work.

To find out more about the complete range of our
publishing, please visit us on the World Wide Web at:
www.pearsoned.co.uk

CORPORATE FINANCE

Passnotes

Denzil Watson and Antony Head

Sheffield Hallam University

Financial Times
Prentice Hall
is an imprint of

Harlow, England • London • New York • Boston • San Francisco • Toronto
Sydney • Tokyo • Singapore • Hong Kong • Seoul • Taipei • New Delhi
Cape Town • Madrid • Mexico City • Amsterdam • Munich • Paris • Milan

Pearson Education Limited
Edinburgh Gate
Harlow
Essex CM20 2JE
England

and Associated Companies throughout the world

Visit us on the World Wide Web at:
www.pearsoned.co.uk

First published 2011

© Pearson Education Limited 2011

ISBN: 978-0-273-72526-8

British Library Cataloguing-in-Publication Data
A catalogue record for this book is available from the British Library

Library of Congress Cataloging-in-Publication Data
Watson, Denzil.
    Corporate finance : passnotes / Denzil Watson and Antony Head. -- 1st ed.
        p. cm.
    Includes bibliographical references and index.
    ISBN 978-0-273-72526-8
    1.   Corporations--Finance. I. Head, Antony, 1953- II. Title.
    HG4026.W373 2011
    658.15--dc22

                                        2010041531

10 9 8 7 6 5 4 3 2 1
14 13 12 11 10

Typeset in 8/10pt Helvetica Neue by 30
Printed and bound in Great Britain by Ashford Colour Press Ltd, Gosport, Hampshire

Contents

How to use this book

These *Corporate Finance Passnotes* should be used in conjunction with the 5th edition of *Corporate Finance: Principles and Practice* by Denzil Watson and Antony Head, and all page references relate to that textbook.

The authors have found that students often need help when revising corporate finance in preparation for examinations or assessments. These *Corporate Finance Passnotes* cover the subject matter of every chapter in the textbook in sufficient detail to act as revision notes, giving you vital assistance as you progress through revising this often difficult subject.

The *Corporate Finance Passnotes* can easily be slipped into your pocket and studied when leisure moments arise – for example, on public transport or between teaching sessions. They can also serve as a vital reminder in those last few hours before an examination. The Examination Pointers at the end of each topic should also be useful to you.

The authors recommend that you study these *Corporate Finance Passnotes* at the same time as the textbook so that you are fully aware of how they extract the key information relating to each topic area. The *Corporate Finance Passnotes* are not a substitute for the textbook. To get the maximum benefit from the *Corporate Finance Passnotes* you should return to the textbook whenever you find something you do not understand.

The authors wish you success in your studies.

Acknowledgements

We are grateful to the following for permission to reproduce copyright material:

Figure 9.5 adapted from The cost of capital, corporation finance and the theory of investment *American Economic Review*, Vol. 48, pp. 261–96 (Miller, M. and Modigliani, F. 1958); Figure 9.6 adapted from Taxes and the cost of capital: a correction *American Economic Review*, Vol. 53, pp. 433–43 (Miller, M. and Modigliani, F. 1963).

In some instances we have been unable to trace the owners of copyright material, and we would appreciate any information that would enable us to do so.

1

The finance function

Introduction

Corporate finance is concerned with:

- managing the finances of an organisation efficiently and effectively in order to achieve the organisation's objectives;
- planning and controlling where finance is raised from;
- allocating financial resources.

Two key corporate finance concepts

Risk and return

A key corporate finance concept is that an investor or a company takes on more risk only if a higher return is offered in compensation.

- *Return* refers to the financial rewards gained as a result of making an investment.
- *Risk* refers to the possibility that the actual return may be different from the expected return.

▐ The time value of money

Another key corporate finance concept is that the value of money changes over time. You will always prefer receiving £100 now to receiving £100 in one year's time. Your preference depends on:

- ▪ time;
- ▪ inflation;
- ▪ risk.

▐ Compounding

This determines the *future value* of a sum of money invested now where interest is left in the account after it has been paid, i.e. interest is earned on interest in future years.

$$FV = C_0(1 + i)^n$$

where: FV = future value
C_0 = sum deposited now
i = interest rate
n = number of years until the cash flow occurs.

▐ Discounting

This is the opposite of compounding. It takes us backward from the *future value* of a cash flow to its *present value* by applying an appropriate *discount rate* to the future value.

$$PV = \frac{FV}{(1 + i)^n}$$

where: PV = present value
FV = future value
i = discount rate
n = number of years until the cash flow occurs.

- ▪ Present value factors (discount factors) can be used to discount one-off cash flows.
- ▪ Cumulative present value factors (annuity factors) can be used to find the present value of a series of regular payments of a fixed amount of money over a finite period.

■ The present value of a regular payment of a fixed amount of money over an infinite period of time (a perpetuity) is equal to the payment divided by the discount rate.

Three decision areas

There are three decision areas of corporate finance (see Figure 1.1):

■ investment decisions;
■ financing decisions;
■ dividend decisions.

Investment: company decides to take on a large number of attractive new investment projects	**Finance**: company will need to raise finance in order to take up projects	**Dividends**: if finance is not available from external sources, dividends may need to be cut in order to increase internal financing
Dividends: company decides to pay higher levels of dividends to its shareholders	**Finance**: lower level of retained earnings available for investment means company may have to find finance from external sources	**Investment**: if finance is not available from external sources the company may have to postpone future investment projects
Finance: company finances itself using more expensive sources, resulting in a higher cost of capital	**Investment**: due to a higher cost of capital the number of projects attractive to the company decreases	**Dividends**: the company's ability to pay dividends in the future will be adversely affected

Figure 1.1 The interrelationship between investment, financing and dividend decisions

Corporate objectives

The primary financial objective of corporate finance should be to maximise the value of the company for its owners, i.e. the maximisation of shareholder wealth.

- Shareholders receive wealth increases via dividends and capital gains.
- Shareholder wealth will be maximised if dividends and capital gains are maximised.

Companies must consider the views of stakeholders other than shareholders and may adopt one or several substitute objectives over shorter periods. Other corporate objectives include:

- profit maximisation;
- sales maximisation;
- survival;
- social responsibility.

How is shareholder wealth maximised?

Shareholder wealth is directly affected by:

- the magnitude of corporate cash flows;
- the timing of corporate cash flows;
- the risk of corporate cash flows.

The company's ordinary share price is usually taken as a measure of shareholder wealth.

- The share price reflects expected future dividend payments and the long-term prospects of the company.
- The objective of maximising the current market price of the company is used as a substitute for maximising shareholder wealth.
- The share price reflects the NPV of the company's investment decisions.

Shareholder wealth can be maximised by making good investment, financing and dividend decisions, including:

- using NPV to assess projects and accepting all projects with a positive NPV;
- raising finance in proportions that minimise a company's cost of capital;
- adopting the most appropriate dividend policy;
- managing a company's working capital efficiently;
- identifying, assessing and managing risks faced by a company.

The agency problem

The agency problem occurs when managers make decisions that are not consistent with the objective of shareholder wealth maximisation. There are three reasons for the agency problem:

- separation of ownership and control;
- differing goals of managers and shareholders;
- asymmetry of information.

Examples of possible management goals include:

- corporate growth, or maximising the size of the company;
- increasing managerial power;
- creating job security;
- increasing managerial pay and rewards;
- pursuing personal objectives or pet projects.

A company can be viewed as a series of agency relationships (the connecting arrows in Figure 1.2).

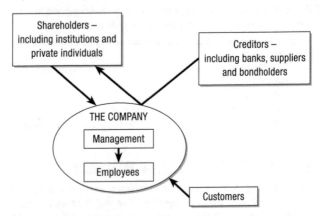

Figure 1.2 The agency relationships that exist between the various stakeholders of a company

▊ Signs of an agency problem

- Managerial reward schemes are based on short-term performance measures.
- Managers use the payback method when appraising possible projects.
- Managers make investments to diversify risk in order to safeguard their own jobs.
- Managers undertake low-risk projects when shareholders prefer higher-risk projects.
- Managers use equity finance rather than debt finance.

■ Dealing with the agency problem

In order to reduce the agency problem, shareholders could monitor the actions of managers.

- ■ The benefits of more optimal managerial behaviour must exceed the costs of monitoring.
- ■ Smaller investors may allow larger shareholders to incur the bulk of monitoring costs.

In order to reduce the agency problem, incentives may be given to managers, such as:

- ■ performance-related pay (although it is difficult to find a good performance measure);
- ■ executive share option schemes (although share prices can move independently of corporate decisions).

Directors can be voted out of office by shareholders.

■ The agency problem between debt holders and shareholders

Debt holders can protect their investment in a company by:

- ■ securing their debt against the company's assets;
- ■ inserting restrictive covenants into debt finance issue documents.

■ The influence of institutional investors

- ■ Institutional shareholders account for a significant proportion of UK-listed shares.
- ■ Institutional investors can put pressure on companies to maintain their dividends.
- ■ Institutional investors are becoming more interested in corporate governance issues.

■ The influence of international investors

- International investors now account for the ownership of two in five of UK-listed shares.
- They have increased their market share at the expense of domestic pension funds, insurance companies and individual investors.
- It is therefore more difficult for companies to identify and understand shareholder needs.

▌ Corporate governance

In the UK, corporate governance problems have been tackled through self-regulation.

- Regulation seeks to promote fairness and transparency in corporate activity through internal controls and the role of financial reporting and accountability.
- The Combined Code is overseen by the London Stock Exchange, which includes compliance with the provisions of the Code in its listing requirements.
- The Code stresses the importance of:
  1 companies having a balanced board structure;
  2 independent non-executive directors linking the board and shareholders;
  3 shareholder vigilance in solving governance problem.
- The US Sarbanes–Oxley Act established strong standards for all US public companies.

(Vignette 1.3 on p. 21 in the textbook illustrates some key issues in corporate governance.)

Examination pointers

✔ Examination questions often assume that you have a good understanding of the link between risk and return.

✔ Discounting and present values are used in many areas of corporate finance, so ensure that this is a technique you have mastered.

✔ The objective of maximising shareholder wealth is often referred to when assessing financial decisions – for example, by looking at capital gains and share price changes.

✔ Agency and corporate governance are usually covered in essay questions.

2

Capital markets, market efficiency and ratio analysis

Introduction

Capital markets are places where:

- companies can raise equity finance and debt finance;
- investors can buy and sell company and government securities.

Companies and investors want capital markets to price their shares and bonds fairly. Companies and investors need information to make financial decisions, and this can be provided by the financial media and by ratio analysis.

Sources of business finance

One source is internal finance, such as retained earnings (surplus cash) and efficiency savings. Other sources are external finance such as equity and short-term or long-term debt (Figure 2.1).

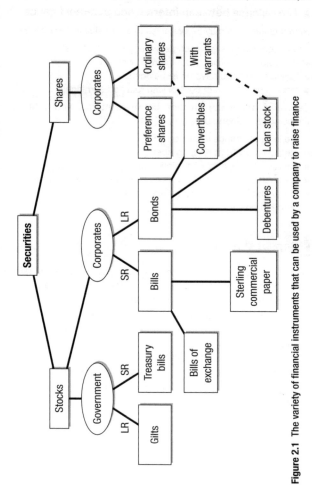

Figure 2.1 The variety of financial instruments that can be used by a company to raise finance

■ The balance between internal and external finance

Retained earnings may be preferred to external finance because:

- retained earnings are seen as a ready source of cash;
- the dividend decision is an internal one;
- retained earnings have no issue costs;
- there is no dilution of control with retained earnings.

Decisions about the balance between internal and external financing will depend on:

- the level of finance required;
- the cash flow from existing operations;
- the opportunity cost of retained earnings;
- the costs associated with raising external finance;
- the availability of external sources of finance;
- dividend policy.

Capital markets

Capital markets are where companies and governments can raise cash (primary market) and where long-term financial securities can be bought and sold (secondary market).

- The secondary market provides pricing information and liquidity.
- The London Stock Exchange (LSE) is the main UK market for equity and bonds.
- The Alternative Investment Market (AIM) is less regulated and is mainly for the shares of small and growing companies.

(Data on capital markets is given in Tables 2.1 and 2.2 on pp. 35–6 in the textbook.)

Capital market efficiency

This can be divided into:

- operational efficiency (transaction costs are low and trading is quick);
- pricing efficiency (security prices fully and fairly reflect all relevant information);
- allocational efficiency (the pricing mechanism allocates funds to their best uses).

The efficient market hypothesis states that the prices of securities fully and fairly reflect all relevant available information (Fama 1970).

■ Weak form efficiency

Security prices reflect all historical information, so abnormal gains cannot be made by using technical analysis (chartism). Empirical evidence suggests that most capital markets are weak form efficient. Security prices should move randomly (random walk) as new information arrives randomly and its nature cannot be predicted.

■ Weak form tests

Statistical tests have been made of weak form efficiency:

- serial correlation tests (e.g. Kendall 1953);
- run tests (e.g. Fama 1965);
- filter tests (e.g. Alexander 1961).

Recent studies show that:

- Weak form efficiency is still broadly supported (Megginson 1997; Beechey et al. 2000);
- Emerging capital markets may be weak form inefficient (e.g. Magnus 2008).

■ Semi-strong form efficiency

Security prices reflect all past information and all publicly available information, and react quickly and accurately to new information. Abnormal returns cannot be made by using fundamental analysis. Empirical evidence suggests that most capital markets are semi-strong form efficient.

■ Semi-strong form tests

Event studies look at the speed and accuracy of security price responses to new information.

- Event studies support the view that capital markets are semi-strong form efficient.
- Event studies offer evidence of anomalies (e.g. Beechey *et al*. 2000).

■ Strong form efficiency

Security prices reflect all information, whether public or not, therefore abnormal gains cannot be made by any investor. Empirical evidence suggests that capital markets are not strong form efficient.

■ Strong form tests

- Capital markets are not strong form efficient because insider trading can occur.
- Strong form efficiency can only be tested indirectly (e.g. assessing experts' performance).

■ Implications of the efficient market hypothesis

For investors:

- paying for investment research has no value;
- studying published accounts and investment tips has no value;
- there are no bargains on the stock market.

For a company and its managers:

- the focus should be on making financial decisions that increase shareholder wealth;
- manipulation of accounting information will not mislead the market;
- the timing of new issues of shares is not important.

■ Anomalies in the behaviour of share prices

Anomalies that have been reported and investigated include:

- calendar effects;
- size anomalies;
- value effects.

■ Behavioural finance

- Investors do not appear to consistently make wealth-maximising decisions.
- Psychological factors can influence investor decisions.
- Irrational investor behaviour can have significant effects on share price movements.

Assessing financial performance

A wide range of stakeholders is interested in the analysis of financial performance:

- shareholders;
- investors;
- company managers.

■ Profit, EBITDA and cash

Some of the deficiencies of accounting profit can be remedied by using earnings before interest, tax, depreciation and amortisation (EBITDA), which is similar to cash flow from operating activities, ignoring the effect of changes in working capital.

- EBITDA eliminates financing and capital expenditure effects, and can thus indicate trends in sustainable profitability.
- EBITDA can be compared with capital employed.
- EBITDA can be criticised as a measure of cash flow because it uses earnings.
- EBITDA ignores the contribution to cash flow made by changes in working capital.

■ The need for benchmarks

Performance measures and accounting ratios must be compared with benchmarks such as:

- financial targets set by a company's strategic plan;
- performance measures and ratios of companies with similar business activities;
- average performance measures and ratios for the company's business sector;
- performance measures and ratios for the company from previous years.

■ Categories of ratios

- Profitability ratios
- Activity ratios
- Liquidity ratios
- Gearing ratios
- Investor ratios.

The golden rule is *always* to compare like with like.

■ Profitability ratios

(Illustrations of calculations of all the following ratios are given on pp. 48–57 in the textbook.)

Return on capital employed (ROCE)

$$\frac{\text{Profit before interest and tax} \times 100}{\text{Capital employed}}$$

This ratio relates the overall profitability to the finance used to generate it, and there is a close link between ROCE and accounting rate of return.

Net profit margin

$$\frac{\text{Profit before interest and tax} \times 100}{\text{Sales or turnover}}$$

This ratio indicates cost control efficiency in generating profit from sales, and a fall in ROCE may be due to a fall in net profit margin.

Net asset turnover

$$\frac{\text{Sales or turnover}}{\text{Capital employed}}$$

This ratio gives a guide to productive efficiency and a fall in ROCE may be due to a fall in asset turnover rather than a fall in net profit margin.

Gross profit margin

$$\frac{\text{Gross profit} \times 100}{\text{Sales and turnover}}$$

This ratio shows how well costs of production have been controlled.

EBITDA/capital employed

$$\frac{\text{EBITDA} \times 100}{\text{Capital employed}}$$

This ratio relates EBITDA to the equity and debt finance used to generate it.

■ Activity ratios

Activity ratios show how efficiently a company has managed its short-term assets and liabilities.

Trade receivables days or trade receivables ratio

$$\frac{\text{Trade receivables} \times 365}{\text{Credit sales}}$$

This ratio gives the average period of credit being taken by customers.

Trade payables days or trade payables ratio

$$\frac{\text{Trade payables} \times 365}{\text{Cost of sales}}$$

This ratio gives the average time taken for suppliers of goods and services to be paid.

Inventory days or inventory turnover

$$\frac{\text{Stock or inventory} \times 365}{\text{Cost of sales}}$$

This ratio shows how long it takes a company to turn its inventories into sales. The shorter the inventory days ratio, the lower the cost to the company of holding inventory.

Cash conversion cycle

The cash conversion cycle is the sum of inventory days and trade receivables days, less trade payables days.

Non-current asset turnover

$$\frac{\text{Sales or turnover}}{\text{Non-current assets}}$$

This ratio indicates the sales being generated by the non-current assets of a company.

Sales/net working capital

$$\frac{\text{Sales or turnover}}{\text{Net current assets}}$$

This ratio shows the level of working capital supporting sales and it can be used to forecast the level of working capital needed for a given level of sales.

■ Liquidity ratios

Current ratio

$$\frac{\text{Current assets}}{\text{Current liabilities}}$$

This ratio measures the ability of the company to meet its financial obligations as they fall due.

Quick ratio

$$\frac{\text{Current assets less stock}}{\text{Current liabilities}}$$

This ratio compares liquid current assets with short-term liabilities.

■ Gearing ratios

Capital gearing ratio

$$\frac{\text{Long-term debt} \times 100}{\text{Capital employed}}$$

This ratio shows the proportion of debt finance used by a company.

- It is usual in corporate finance to calculate gearing using market values for debt and equity.
- Reserves are not included in the calculation of the market value of equity.

Debt/equity ratio

$$\frac{\text{Long-term debt} \times 100}{\text{Share capital and reserves}}$$

This ratio serves a similar purpose to capital gearing.

Interest coverage ratio

$$\frac{\text{Profit before interest and tax}}{\text{Interest charges}}$$

This ratio shows how many times a company can cover its interest payment. A value of more than seven times is usually regarded as safe.

▌ Investor ratios

Return on equity (ROE)

$$\frac{\text{Earnings after tax and preference dividends}}{\text{Shareholders' funds}}$$

ROE compares profit after tax with the book value of shareholders' funds.

Dividend per share

$$\frac{\text{Total dividend paid to ordinary shareholders}}{\text{Number of issued ordinary shares}}$$

Earnings per share

$$\frac{\text{Earnings after tax and preference dividends}}{\text{Number of issued ordinary shares}}$$

This is seen as a key ratio by stock market investors.

Dividend cover

$$\frac{\text{Earnings per share}}{\text{Dividend per share}}$$

This ratio offers a margin of safety as far as dividend payments are concerned.

Price/earnings ratio

$$\frac{\text{Market price per share}}{\text{Earnings per share}}$$

This is also seen as a key ratio by stock market investors and it can therefore indicate the confidence of investors in the future performance of a company. It can also be used to value a company's shares.

Payout ratio

$$\frac{\text{Total dividend paid to ordinary shareholders} \times 100}{\text{Earnings after tax and preference dividends}}$$

This ratio is often used in the analysis of dividend policy.

Dividend yield

$$\frac{\text{Dividend per share} \times 100}{\text{Market price of share}}$$

This ratio gives a measure of the dividend return on an investment.

Earnings yield

$$\frac{\text{Earnings per share} \times 100}{\text{Market price of share}}$$

This ratio gives a measure of the earnings return on an investment and it is the reciprocal of the price/earnings ratio.

■ Earnings yield can be used as a discount rate in company valuation.

■ Problems with ratio analysis

■ The financial position statement relates to a company's position on one day of the year.
■ It can be difficult to find a similar company as a basis for inter-company comparisons.
■ The reliability of ratio analysis depends on the reliability of the information it uses.

∎ Economic profit and economic value added (EVA®)

∎ Economic profit includes an opportunity cost for capital employed in assessing performance:

$$\text{Economic profit} = [\text{Operating profit} \times (1 - t)] - (K_0 \times \text{CE})$$

where: t = company taxation rate
K_0 = average rate of return required by investors
CE = book value of capital employed.

The difficulty of extracting a fair value for invested capital from financial statements is addressed by the performance measure known as EVA:

∎ EVA was trademarked and introduced by the Stern Stewart company in the 1990s.
∎ It gives an overall measure of company performance that focuses attention on the drivers that create shareholder wealth.
∎ EVA makes changes to invested capital and operating profit after tax, and corrects the effect of financial accounting rules that ignore how a company creates shareholder value.

EVA can be defined as:

$$\text{EVA} = [\text{AOP}\,(1 - t)] - (\text{WACC} \times \text{AVIC})$$

where: AOP = adjusted operating profit
t = company taxation rate
WACC = weighted average cost of capital *(see p. 263 in the textbook)*
AVIC = adjusted value of invested capital.

EVA points to the following value-creating strategies:

∎ look for ways to increase net operating profit after tax without increasing capital invested;
∎ invest in projects expected to give returns higher than the company's cost of capital;
∎ take steps to reduce the opportunity cost of the capital invested in the company.

Examination pointers

✔ Make sure you have a good understanding of the wide variety of sources of finance available to a company.

✔ Learn the differences between the three forms of capital market efficiency in terms of the information reflected in share prices and the tests carried out on capital markets.

✔ Note the implications of capital market efficiency for investors and companies, and the need for the different perspective provided by behavioural finance.

✔ Make sure, through repeated practice, that you can calculate all the accounting ratios and that you can interpret their significance from an analysis point of view.

✔ Be prepared to explain the reason for the development of economic value added.

3

Short-term finance and the management of working capital

Introduction

Working capital management is concerned with managing short-term assets and liabilities:

- net working capital is the difference between current assets and current liabilities;
- liquidity refers to the level of cash a company has available;
- working capital management is a key factor in a company's long-term success.

The objectives of working capital management

The objectives of working capital management are profitability and liquidity. Profitability is needed to achieve the objective of maximising shareholder wealth, while liquidity is needed to support the day-to-day operation of a company.

Working capital policies

Key working capital policy areas relate to:

- the level of working capital investment;
- the way in which working capital is financed.

A company should have working capital policies on the management of inventory, trade receivables, cash and short-term investments. These policies should reflect decisions on:

- the amount of investment in each type of current asset and the way in which current assets are financed;
- the nature of business operations and the credit policies of competitors;
- seasonal variations in demand and supply, and the production cycle of the company.

The level of investment in working capital

Levels of investment are shown in Table 3.1.

Table 3.1 Investment policies (see Figure 3.1)

	Investment policy:		
	Conservative	**Moderate**	**Aggressive**
Level of current assets:	Relatively high	Average	Relatively low
Level of risk:	Relatively low	Average	Relatively high
Profitability:	Relatively low	Average	Relatively high

Working capital policies can be described as aggressive, moderate or conservative only by comparing them with the working capital policies of similar companies.

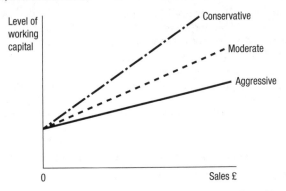

Figure 3.1 Different policies regarding the level of investment in working capital

▌ Short-term finance

- An *overdraft* is an agreement by a bank to allow a company to borrow up to a certain limit. While it is a flexible source of finance, an overdraft is repayable on demand.
- A *short-term bank loan* is for a fixed amount and is repayable in one year or less, with interest on a fixed or floating rate. It is less flexible than an overdraft as interest is payable on the full amount borrowed.
- *Trade credit* is an agreement to pay for goods and services after an agreed period of time, such as 60 days, and is a major source of short-term finance for most companies.

Short-term sources of finance are usually cheaper and more flexible than long-term sources, but are also riskier.

Financing working capital

Corporate assets can be divided into:

- non-current assets (fixed assets);
- permanent current assets (core investment in current assets);
- fluctuating current assets.

Table 3.2 Financing policies (see Figure 3.2)

	Financing policy		
	Conservative	Moderate	Aggressive
Fluctuating current assets financed by:	Short-term and long-term finance	Short-term finance	Short-term finance
Permanent current assets financed by:	Long-term finance	Long-term finance	Short-term and long-term finance
Non-current assets financed by:	Long-term finance	Long-term finance	Long-term finance
Level of risk	Relatively low	Average	Relatively high
Profitability	Relatively low	Average	Relatively high

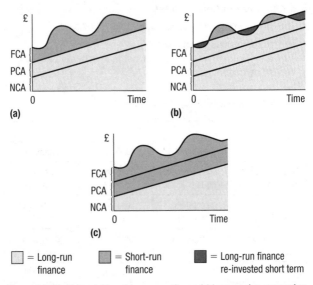

Figure 3.2 The (a) matching, (b) conservative and (c) aggressive approaches to the relative proportions of the long- and short-term debt used to finance working capital

Working capital and the cash conversion cycle

The cash conversion cycle is the period of time between paying for raw materials and receiving payment for goods sold, and can be calculated as inventory days plus trade receivables days, less trade payables days. The longer the cash conversion cycle, the more working capital investment needed.

■ The cash conversion cycle and working capital needs

Forecasts of working capital needs can be based on sales forecasts using the sales/net working capital ratio, and should be reviewed regularly as business activity levels change. Investment in current assets can be reduced by shortening the cash conversion cycle:

- decreasing inventory days (e.g. using Just-in-time methods);
- decreasing trade receivables days (e.g. using an early settlement discount);
- increasing trade payables days (e.g. by negotiating longer credit periods).

Overtrading

Overtrading (undercapitalisation) is where the volume of trade is too large to be supported by the working capital base. It can lead to liquidity problems and even bankruptcy. Overtrading can be caused by:

- a rapid increase in turnover;
- insufficient capital being invested in a new business;
- erosion of a company's capital base.

Overtrading can be cured by:

- introducing new capital (e.g. new equity finance);
- improving working capital management (e.g. chasing late payers);
- reducing business activity (consolidation).

Indications that a company may be overtrading could include:

- rapid sales growth over a relatively short period of time;
- rapid growth in the level of current assets;
- deteriorating inventory days and trade receivables days;
- increasing dependence on short-term finance (e.g. trade finance and leasing);
- declining liquidity (e.g. falling quick ratio).

The management of inventory

The benefits of having inventory must be compared to the costs incurred, including holding costs, replacement costs and inventory costs (see Figure 3.3).

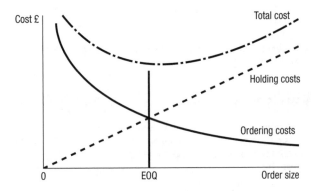

Figure 3.3 The costs of holding stock and the EOQ model

The economic order quantity

The EOQ model calculates an optimum order size by balancing holding costs and inventory costs. It assumes that costs and demand are constant and certain, and it makes no allowance for buffer inventory. The annual holding cost is the average inventory level in units ($Q/2$) multiplied by the holding cost per unit per year (H). The annual ordering cost is the number of orders per year (S/Q) multiplied by the ordering cost per order (F). The total cost (TC) is:

$$TC = \frac{(Q \times H)}{2} + \frac{(S \times F)}{Q}$$

where: Q = order quantity in units
        H = holding cost per unit per year
        S = annual demand in units per year
        F = ordering cost per order.

The minimum total cost occurs when holding costs and ordering costs are equal. Putting holding costs equal to ordering costs and rearranging gives the EOQ formula:

$$Q = \frac{\sqrt{2 \times S \times F}}{H}$$

Q is now the economic order quantity.

Example

Using the EOQ model

If F = €5 per order
      S = 200 000 bars per year
      H = €2.22 per 1000 bars
then: $Q = (2 \times 200\,000 \times 5/(2.22/1000))^{1/2}$
      = 30 015 bars, or approximately 30 boxes
Average inventory level = $Q/2$ = 30 000/2 = 15 000 bars

■ Buffer inventory and lead times

The delay between ordering and delivery is called the lead time. If demand and lead time are constant, a delivery can be ordered when inventory is equal to demand during the lead time. If demand or lead times are uncertain, buffer inventory can be held to guard against running out of inventory.

Figure 3.4 shows inventory levels for a company with a buffer inventory *OB*. Regular orders of size *BQ* are placed, based on average annual demand. Since the lead time is known and is equal to *ab*, new orders are placed when the inventory levels fall to *OR*. Unexpected demand during the lead time can be met from the buffer inventory.

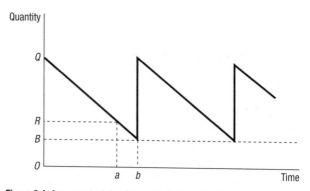

Figure 3.4 Average stock levels, reorder level and buffer stock

■ Just-in-time (JIT) inventory policies

The main purpose of a JIT *purchasing* policy is to minimise the time between delivery and use of the inventory. Such a policy calls for a close relationship between supplier and user. The buyer needs guarantees on quality and reliability of delivery in order to avoid disrupting production. The supplier benefits from long-term purchase agreements. The purchaser benefits from lower holding and handling costs since materials move directly from receipt to production.

The main purpose of a JIT *manufacturing* policy is to minimise inventory between different stages of production. This can be achieved by changing factory layout, reducing the size of production batches and improving production planning.

The management of cash

The amount of cash available must be optimised, interest earned by short-term surplus cash must be maximised, and losses caused by delays in transmitting funds must be minimised. Holding cash incurs an opportunity cost equal to the return that could have been earned if the cash had been invested.

The need for cash

There are three reasons for holding cash:

- transactions motive: cash is held to meet short-term needs and expected cash outflows;
- precautionary motive: cash is held to meet unexpected demands for cash;
- speculative motive: cash reserves held in case an attractive investment opportunity arises.

Optimum cash levels

The optimum cash balance depends on:

- forecasts of future cash inflows and outflows;
- the efficiency of cash management;
- the availability of liquid assets;
- a company's borrowing capability;
- a company's tolerance of risk.

Cash flow problems

Reasons for cash flow problems include:

- making losses;
- inflation;
- overtrading;
- significant items of expenditure (e.g. redemption of debt).

Remedies for cash flow problems include:

- postponing non-essential capital expenditure;
- accelerate cash inflows (e.g. offering early settlement discounts);
- selling short-term investments;
- reducing cash outflows (e.g. cutting dividends).

▮ Cash budgets

Cash budgets are a key tool in managing cash and their preparation helps to control expenditure and to plan borrowing and investment.

▮ Managing cash flows

Cash flows must be managed efficiently:

- debts must be collected when due;
- cash must be banked quickly;
- trade credit should be used when offered;
- float should be minimised.

▮ Investing surplus cash

Short-term cash surpluses must be invested to earn a return, but there must be no risk of capital loss. Default risk should be minimised by diversifying investments. Factors to consider when selecting short-term investments include:

- the size of the short-term cash surplus;
- the ease with which short-term investments can be sold;
- the maturity of the investment;
- the risk and yield of the investment.

Suitable investments include term deposits, sterling certificates of deposit, Treasury bills and sterling commercial paper.

The management of receivables

A receivables management policy should help to maximise expected profits. The nature of the policy will depend on such factors as:

- the usual terms of sale in the company's business sector;
- the company's pricing policy;
- the effectiveness of trade receivables follow-up procedures;
- the administrative costs of debt collection;
- the costs and effects of easing credit.

The policy should balance the benefits gained from offering credit against the costs of doing so. A receivables management policy relies on a *credit analysis system*, a *credit control system* and a *trade receivables collection system*.

■ Credit analysis system

The risk of bad debts can be reduced if customer creditworthiness is checked before credit is granted. Relevant information can be found from a variety of sources, such as bank references, trade references and credit agency reports.

■ Credit control system

The company must ensure that customers keep to their agreed credit limits, while reviewing credit limits on a regular basis. Invoices and statements must be despatched promptly. If a credit limit is exceeded, further transactions should be prevented.

■ Trade receivables collection system

The cost of collecting cash due from trade receivables must be less than the cash received. An aged receivables analysis will identify slow payers and focus managerial attention. Working capital policy will establish procedures for chasing late payers and initiating legal proceedings. Charging interest on overdue accounts may encourage earlier payment.

▌ Insuring against bad debts

Insurance against the risk of bad debts is available on a whole turnover basis or on a specific account basis.

▌ Discounts for early payment

An early settlement discount may encourage early payment, but the benefit of the discount must exceed the cost of the discount.

Example

Evaluating a change in trade receivables policy

Given the following information, is the proposed discount worth introducing?

Annual credit sales: £15m per year (not affected by proposed discount)
Trade receivables days: 90 days
Proposed discount: 2% for payment within 15 days
Proposed credit period: 60 days
Customers taking discount: 60%
Cost of short-term finance: 10% per year

Suggested answer	£000
Current receivables: $15\,000 \times (90/365) =$	3699
Proposed receivables:	
$15\,000 \times [(40\% \times 60) + (60\% \times 15)]/365$	1356
Reduction in receivables	2343
Finance cost saving: $2343 \times 0.10 =$	234.3
Cost of discount: $15\,000 \times 2\% \times 60\% =$	180.0
Net benefit of proposed policy change:	54.3

The policy change is financially attractive.

■ Factoring

A factoring company can:

■ take over sales administration, credit analysis, credit control and receivables collection;

■ accelerate cash inflow by offering a cash advance of up to 80% of receivables;

■ provide bad debt insurance by factoring on a non-recourse basis.

A factor charges a percentage of turnover fee (between 0.5% and 3%) and interest on cash advances. The interest charge can be compared with the cost of short-term borrowing.

The advantages of factoring to a company may include:

■ prompt payment of suppliers and perhaps early payment discounts;

■ a decrease in the amount of working capital tied up in trade receivables;

■ financing growth through sales;

■ savings on sales administration costs;

■ benefits arising from the factor's experience in credit analysis and credit control.

■ Invoice discounting

Invoice discounting involves selling selected invoices to a third party (e.g. a factoring company) while keeping control of the sales ledger. The main cost here is a discount charge, although a percentage of turnover fee may also be levied. Invoice discounting improves cash flows.

Example

Cost–benefit analysis of factoring

Given the following information, is the factor's offer worth accepting?

Current annual credit sales: €4.5m
Current trade receivables days: 50 days
Current bad debts: 4% of credit sales
Annual fee of factor: 1% of credit sales
Cost savings under factor: €35 000 per year
Trade receivables days under factor: 30 days
Bad debts under factor: nil
Advance offered by factor: 80% of receivables at 11% per year
Cost of short-term finance: 10% per year.

Suggested answer	**€000**
Current level of trade receivables: €4.5m × (50/365) =	616.4
Trade receivables under factor: €4.5m × (30/365) =	369.9

	€000
Cost of financing current receivables: 616.4 × 10% =	61.6
Cost of bad debts: 4.5m × 0.4% =	18.0
Costs of current policy:	79.6

Cost of financing receivables under factor	**€000**
€369.9 × [(0.8 × 11%) + (0.2 × 10%)] =	40.0
Factor's annual fee: €4.5m × 0.01 =	45.0
Cost savings under factor:	(35.0)
Cost of financing receivables under factor:	50.0

The factor's offer will save €29 600 per year and so is financially acceptable.

Examination pointers

✔ Working capital management balances liquidity and profitability.

✔ Be prepared to discuss working capital policies and the factors that influence them, such as business operations, the cash conversion cycle, the analysis of current assets, and the risk and cost of short-term and long-term finance.

✔ Overtrading may need to be discussed following a ratio analysis of relevant information.

✔ Make sure that you can calculate the EOQ and discuss the weaknesses of this approach to inventory management compared to more modern approaches such as JIT.

✔ While cash management can be the subject of a discussion question, cash flow forecasting is a key skill in corporate finance.

✔ Receivables management is often a discussion topic, but make sure that you can evaluate a change in credit policy, since this a frequent requirement in examinations.

4

Long-term finance: equity finance

Introduction

Equity finance (ordinary share capital) is:

- the foundation of a company's capital structure;
- the source of most of its long-term finance;
- the basis for obtaining a listing on the stock exchange.

Equity finance

Equity finance is raised by selling ordinary shares to existing shareholders or new investors. Ordinary shares are bought and sold on stock exchanges throughout the world and, like all investors, ordinary shareholders want a satisfactory return on their investment.

- Ordinary shares of a company have a par value (nominal value) and they cannot be issued for less than this value.
- Ordinary shares are usually sold at a premium to par value: the nominal value of issued shares is given by the ordinary share account and the premium on issue is given by the share premium account.

■ The rights of ordinary shareholders

Shareholder rights include:

- the right to attend general meetings of the company;
- the right to vote on the appointment of directors;
- the right to vote on the appointment and remuneration of auditors;
- the right to receive the Annual Report of the company;
- the right to receive a share of any dividend agreed;
- the right to receive a share of any assets remaining after a company is liquidated;
- the right to participate in a new issue of ordinary shares (the pre-emptive right).

Equity finance, risk and return

Ordinary shareholders are the ultimate bearers of the risk associated with corporate business activities because they are at the bottom of the creditor hierarchy. Ordinary shareholders therefore expect a greater return than other providers of finance. The order of precedence in the creditor hierarchy is as follows:

- secured creditors;
- unsecured creditors;
- preference shareholders;
- ordinary shareholders.

The stock exchange

The London Stock Exchange is a market for ordinary shares and bonds. Trading on the London Stock Exchange is regulated by the Financial Services Authority in its role as the UK Listing Authority (UKLA). The responsibilities of the UKLA include:

- admitting securities to listing;
- maintaining the Official List;

- regulating sponsors;
- imposing and enforcing continuing obligations on issuing companies;
- suspending and cancelling listings where necessary.

■ The new equity issues market

Companies wanting a listing on the London Stock Exchange (LSE) or the Alternative Investment Market (AIM) must appoint (a) a *broker* to advise on an issue price and to market the issue to investors, and (b) a *sponsor* to help with meeting regulations, putting out a prospectus, managing the listing process and liaising with the UKLA and the LSE.

■ New issue methods

Placing

Ordinary shares are issued at a fixed price to institutional investors. The issue is underwritten by the issuing company's sponsor. A placing is a relatively low-risk issue method and so has a low cost compared to a public offer.

Public offer

Ordinary shares are issued at a fixed price to the public with the help of the sponsor and the broker. This method is used for large issues and gives a wide spread of ownership. The issue is underwritten and so the issuing company is guaranteed the finance it needs.

Introduction

Here, a listing is granted to the ordinary shares of a company which already satisfies the listing regulations. No new shares are sold and no new finance is raised.

■ Listing regulations

Some of the requirements of the UKLA Listing Rules are as follows:

- audited published accounts, usually for at least three years prior to admission;
- at least 25% of the company's shares must be in public hands;
- the company must be able to conduct its business independently of controlling interests;
- the company must publish a prospectus containing a forecast of expected performance;
- the company must have a minimum market capitalisation of £700 000.

■ Relative importance of placing and public offer

In recent years, a public offer has been the most frequent method of raising cash on the LSE, while placings are used more frequently in smaller markets, such as the AIM.

(Table 4.2 on p. 103 in the textbook illustrates the relative importance of the two methods.)

■ Underwriting

Companies insure against new equity issues being unsuccessful through underwriting.

- The main underwriter will appoint sub-underwriters.
- The underwriting fee is about 2% to 3% of the proceeds of the new issue.

■ Advantages of obtaining a stock exchange quotation

There are several benefits of becoming listed on a stock exchange which may encourage a company to seek a listing.

Raising finance through coming to market

- Owners of a company can sell some of their shares and so realise some of their investment.

43

- Venture capitalists can use a listing as an exit route from their investment.
- A company can, for example, raise funds for a business expansion.

Access to finance

- A listed company will have easier access to external sources of equity capital than an unlisted company.
- The credibility and reputation of a listed company will make it easier to raise new debt at a lower cost than an unlisted company.

Uses of shares

- The shares of a listed company are more likely to be acceptable in financing an acquisition, since they have a ready market.

▍ Disadvantages of obtaining a stock exchange quotation

For a balanced view, the disadvantages of a stock exchange listing should be considered.

Costs of a quotation

- Obtaining and maintaining a stock exchange quotation is costly;
- one of these costs is the cost of increased financial disclosure.

Shareholder expectations

- The directors of a newly-listed company will need to consider the expectations of new shareholders, including institutional shareholders;
- the risk of being taken over increases if shareholder expectations are not met.

Rights issues

A company must offer new ordinary shares to existing shareholders (a rights issue), unless they have waived their pre-emptive right. Existing patterns of ownership and control are preserved as new shares are offered on a pro rata basis, e.g. a 1 for 4 issue.

- Rights issues are cheaper than a public offer;
- the rights issue price is at a discount to the current market price, e.g. 15% to 20%;
- the cum rights price is the share price before the new issue takes place;
- the ex-rights price is the market price after the rights issue has occurred.

The theoretical ex-rights price

This share price is a weighted average of the cum rights price and the rights issue price:

$$P_e = P_P \frac{N_O}{N} + P_N \frac{N_N}{N}$$

where: P_e = the theoretical ex-rights price
P_P = cum rights price
P_N = rights issue price
N_O = number of old shares
N_N = number of new shares
N = the total number of shares.

The value of the rights

Rights attached to shares can be sold to other investors. The value of the rights is the gain the buyer could make by exercising them. This is the difference between the theoretical ex-rights price and the rights issue price.

Example

Calculation of the theoretical ex-rights price

Number of shares in issue before rights issue:	2 million ordinary shares
Cum rights price:	£2.10 per share
Rights issue price:	£1.85 per share
Rights issue terms:	1 for 4 issue
New shares issued:	0.5 million shares

Theoretical ex-rights price =
$$[(2m \times 2.10) + (0.5m \times 1.85)]/2.5m = £2.05$$

Alternatively, using the terms of the 1 for 4 rights issue:

Theoretical ex-rights price =
$$[(4 \times 2.10) + (1 \times 1.85)]/5 = £2.05$$

Value of the rights = 2.05 − 1.85 = 20p per new share or 5p per existing share.

∎ Rights issues and shareholder wealth

Shareholder wealth is not be affected by a rights issue, provided shareholders either subscribe for the issue or sell their rights. If investing the cash raised gives a share price higher than the theoretical ex-rights price, shareholder wealth increases.

Example

Wealth effect of a rights issue

Cum rights price:	£2.10 per share
Rights issue price:	£1.85 per share
Rights issue terms:	1 for 4 issue
New shares issued:	0.5 million shares
Theoretical ex-rights price:	£2.05 per share
Value of the rights:	5p per existing share
Shareholder owns 1000 shares	

Buy 250 new shares

Current value of shares =	£2100 (1000 × £2.10)
Cash for 250 new shares =	£462.50 (250 × £1.85)
Value of 1250 shares ex-rights =	£2562.50 (1250 × £2.05)

Shareholder wealth is unchanged, although some wealth has changed from cash into shares.

Sell rights attached to 250 shares

Value of 1000 shares ex-rights =	£2050 (1000 × £2.05)
Cash from sale of rights =	£50 (1000 × £0.05)
Wealth position after rights issue =	£2100

Shareholder wealth is unchanged, although some wealth has changed from shares into cash.

Take no action over rights issue

Current value of shares =	£2100 (1000 × £2.10)
Value of 1000 shares ex-rights =	£2050 (1000 × £2.05)

Shareholder wealth has fallen by £50 as the share price has moved from cum rights to ex rights.

∎ Market price after a rights issue

The actual ex-rights price will depend on:

- investor expectations about the future state of the economy;
- investors opinions on the proposed use of the new funds by the company;
- the expected level of dividends per share;
- the earnings yield on the new funds raised.

The ex-rights price (P_e) will depend on the expected earnings yield on the new funds raised (γ_N) and the earnings yield on existing funds (γ_o):

$$P_e = P_P \frac{N_O}{N} + P_N \frac{N_N \gamma_N}{N \gamma_o}$$

where:
P_P = cum rights price
P_N = rights issue price
N_O = number of old shares
N_N = number of new shares
N = total number of shares
γ_N/γ_O = ratio of earnings yield on new capital to earnings yield on old capital.

If γ_N/γ_O is more than 1, the predicted ex-rights share price will be higher than the theoretical ex-rights price.

Empirical evidence suggests that the theoretical ex-rights price is a reasonably accurate predictor of the actual ex-rights price per share.

■ Underwriting and deep discount rights issues

Even though shareholder wealth is not affected by a rights issue, and the discount to the current market price serves only to maintain the desirability of the rights issue in the event of a fall in the share price in the market, rights issue are still underwritten. Furthermore, even though the size of the discount is irrelevant, deep discount rights issues are rare.

Scrip issues, share splits, scrip dividends, share repurchases

■ Scrip issues and share splits

A *scrip issue* (bonus issue) is a conversion of existing reserves into additional shares, distributed pro rata to existing shareholders.

A *share split* (stock split) reduces the nominal value of each share and simultaneously increases the number of shares in issue, so that the value of the shares in the financial position statement is unchanged (e.g. each 50p share is replaced by five 10p shares). A share split can increase the liquidity of shares on the stock market and may have a positive effect on shareholder wealth.

■ Scrip dividends

This is an offer of ordinary shares as a partial or total alternative to a cash dividend, which is treated as income by the tax authorities. Benefits to the company include:

■ a decrease in cash flow if the scrip dividend is taken up;
■ a small decrease in gearing;
■ little (if any) change in the share price.

Ordinary shareholders can benefit by an increased shareholding without incurring dealing costs.

■ Share repurchases

A UK company can buy back its own shares provided that its shareholders have given permission. Reasons for buying back shares include:

■ shareholders may be able to invest a cash surplus more effectively than the company;
■ the value of remaining shares will be enhanced after a share repurchase, since there is a negligible increase in financial risk and hence little change in the cost of equity;
■ return on capital employed (ROCE) will increase;
■ earnings per share will increase.

Preference shares

These shares give the right to receive a share of after-tax profits (a dividend) before ordinary shareholders and have the following features:

■ ordinary dividends cannot be paid until all preference dividends have been paid;
■ preference shares are higher in the creditor hierarchy than ordinary shares;
■ preference shareholders receive any proceeds of liquidation before ordinary shareholders;

- preference shares are less risky than ordinary shares;
- preference shares are treated as prior charge capital when calculating gearing.

However, preference shares are riskier than debt, for several reasons:

- preference shares are not secured on company assets;
- preference dividends cannot be paid until interest payments have been made;
- debt holders receive any proceeds of liquidation before preference share holders.

Preference shares may be cumulative (unpaid dividends are rolled forward to be paid in the future) or non-cumulative, and participating (receive a percentage of profits if they exceed a given level) or non-participating.

■ Variable rate preference shares

There are two kinds of variable rate preference shares:

- shares where the dividend rate is linked to a variable market rate (such as LIBOR);
- shares where the dividend rate is adjusted to keep the market value constant (e.g. AMPS).

■ Convertible preference shares

These preference shares give the holder the option to convert them into ordinary shares at a future date.

■ The popularity of preference shares

Preference shares are unpopular since they are more expensive to a company than debt, which requires a lower return as it is less risky to an investor, and which is also tax efficient. Venture capital financing, however, may include convertible redeemable preference shares.

■ The advantages and disadvantages of preference shares

Advantages of preference shares include:

- dividends do not need to be paid if profits are not enough to cover them (unless they are cumulative preference shares);
- they do not carry general voting rights and so will not dilute ownership and control;
- they preserve debt capacity, as they are not secured;
- there is no right to appoint a receiver if preference dividends are not paid.

The major disadvantage of preference shares to companies is their higher cost relative to the cost of debt.

Examination pointers

Key examination points include:

✔ Make sure you understand the creditor hierarchy and the risk–return relationship that underlies the relative returns of different sources of finance.

✔ You must be able to explain the key features of a capital market and the new issue market.

✔ Calculating the theoretical ex-rights price can be a key step in evaluating the relative merit to a company of different sources of finance.

✔ Preference shares can be confusing because they pay dividends but are often treated as debt, for example, in calculating gearing.

5

Long-term finance: debt finance, hybrid finance and leasing

Introduction

Long-term debt finance is very different from equity finance.

- Interest on long-term debt is an allowable deduction against taxable profit, but dividends paid on equity finance are a share of after-tax profit.
- Interest on debt must be paid, but dividends may be missed if managers so decide.
- Debt holders are paid off before shareholders in a corporate liquidation.
- Long-term debt is therefore less risky than equity finance and so requires a lower return.

Leasing can be compared with borrowing as a source of finance.

Bonds, loan stock and debentures

Bonds have a UK par value of £100 and the interest paid is a percentage of the par value. The interest rate paid is reduced by the tax efficiency of debt, for example if profit tax is 30% then interest on a 10% bond is effectively reduced to 7% [i.e. $10 \times (1 - 0.3)$].

The principal (i.e. par value) on redeemable debt is repaid on the redemption date.

- A debenture is usually a secured bond while loan stock is an unsecured bond. Key contract details relating to the bond are contained in the bond issue document.
- Bonds may be secured by either a fixed charge (on specified assets) or by a floating charge (on a class of assets).

Restrictive covenants

Restrictive (or negative) covenants prevent any significant change in the *risk profile* of the company relative to the issue date, for example by:

- limiting the amount of additional debt that can be issued by the company;
- giving a maximum gearing ratio;
- specifying a minimum level of interest cover;
- specifying a target range for the current ratio.

If the restrictive covenant is breached, the bond holders can take action to recover their funds.

Redemption and refinancing

The significant cash flow demand caused by redemption of a bond issue can be provided for by saving regularly into a sinking fund. Alternatively, a company can *refinance* by replacing an issue of bonds due for redemption with a new issue of long-term debt or a new issue of equity. Refinancing allows a company to:

- maintain the matching of long-term assets with long-term liabilities;
- change the amount, the maturity or the nature of existing debt in line with a company's financial strategy.

Companies can also use a redemption window, a call option on the bond issue, or redemption at a premium to par in order to gain early redemption.

■ Floating interest rates

Floating or variable interest rates can be linked to, for example, London Interbank Offered Rate (LIBOR) or bank base rate, and may be attractive to:

- investors who either want a return comparable with prevailing market interest rates or want protection against unanticipated inflation;
- companies who want to hedge against falling interest rates.

■ Bond ratings

Bond ratings measure investment risk as regards interest payments and repayment of principal, and are provided by commercial organisations such as Moody's Investor Service. Institutional investors usually invest only in investment-grade bonds, so a downgrading to non-investment grade will lead to an increase in a bond's required return and a fall in its market price.

■ Deep discount and zero coupon bonds

A deep discount bond is issued at a deep discount to par in exchange for a lower interest rate and redemption at par (or a premium to par). Deep discount bonds will be attractive to:

- investors who prefer capital gains to interest income, since these can be taxed differently;
- companies who expect most of the income from an investment to occur later in its life.

A zero coupon bond pays no interest at all and hence offers a return only in the form of capital appreciation. Zero coupon bonds have similar attractions to deep discount bonds.

■ New issues

Debt finance is raised in the new issues market (the primary market) through a lead bank, in a process known as book building, perhaps on a syndicated basis in order to spread risk.

(Several vignettes illustrating the features of bonds are given on pp. 128–131 in the textbook.)

Bank and institutional debt

Long-term loans are available at both fixed and floating interest rates, and on both a fixed and floating charge basis. The cost of bank loans is usually a floating rate linked to the bank base rate. A *repayment schedule* is often agreed between the bank and the borrower, with equal annual payments including both interest and capital. The problems faced by small businesses in raising debt finance can be partially mitigated by government assistance.

(The example on p. 132 in the textbook shows how to calculate the interest element of bank loan repayments.)

International debt finance

Foreign currency borrowing can be used by a company to:

- hedge against exchange rate losses;
- take advantage of comparatively low interest rates;
- diminish the effect of restrictions on currency exchange.

Eurobonds

Eurobonds are bonds outside the control of the country in whose currency they are denominated and are sold in different countries at the same time by large companies and governments. Features of Eurobonds include:

- interest, whether fixed or floating, is payable gross (i.e. before tax);
- interest is lower than on domestic bonds as the Eurobond market is less tightly regulated;
- Eurobond maturities are typically of 5 to 15 years;
- they are bearer securities, so they offer anonymity to their owners;
- they are unsecured and hence are issued by companies with excellent credit ratings.

Convertible bonds

These bonds convert into ordinary shares at the option of the holder on a specified date and at a specified rate. If not converted, they are redeemed on a specified date, which is usually several years after the conversion date. The conversion ratio is the number of ordinary shares obtained from one bond. Conversion terms may vary over time to encourage conversion.

- *Conversion value* is the conversion ratio multiplied by the market price per ordinary share and is the equity market value into which one bond may be converted.
- The *conversion premium* is the difference between the market price of a convertible bond and its conversion value. As conversion approaches, the conversion premium becomes zero.
- The *floor value* of a convertible bond is equal to its value as an ordinary bond with the same interest rate, maturity and risk.
- The *rights premium* is the difference between the market value of a convertible bond and its floor value.

The interest on a convertible bond is less than on an ordinary bond due to the value of the conversion rights. The *actual* market value of a convertible bond depends on:

- the current conversion value;
- the time to conversion;
- the expected conversion value;
- whether the market expects that conversion is likely.

▌ The attractions of convertible bonds to companies

Convertible bonds have a number of attractions to companies:

- companies avoid redemption problems as conversion makes these bonds self-liquidating;
- companies may issue convertible bonds when the company's ordinary share price is seen as depressed or in order to avoid diluting earnings per share;

- they pay fixed interest, aiding financial forecasting and planning;
- interest rates on convertible bonds are lower than on similar ordinary bonds;
- interest payments are tax deductible, lowering the overall cost of capital;
- higher gearing may be possible using convertible debt;
- debt capacity is enhanced on conversion.

Convertibles may have the following disadvantages:

- gearing and financial risk will be increased while convertible bonds are outstanding;
- dilution of the control of existing shareholders will occur on conversion;
- dilution of earnings per share may occur on conversion.

▌ The attractions of convertible bonds to investors

Investors may be attracted to convertible bonds because:

- they offer a lower risk investment in the short term with greater gains potentially in the longer term, i.e. the opportunity to participate financially in the growth of the company;
- they allow bond holders to evaluate the performance of a company before deciding to become shareholders.

▌ Warrants

Warrants give the right to buy new ordinary shares at a future date (the exercise date) at a fixed price (the exercise price). They are usually attached to unsecured bonds as an *equity sweetener* and can be sold on into the warrants market.

- The *intrinsic value* of a warrant (V_w) is the current share price (P) less the exercise price (E), multiplied by the number of shares obtained for each warrant exercised (N):

$$V_w = (P - E) \times N$$

- The *time value* of a warrant reflects the possibility of future share price growth. The actual warrant price will be the sum of the intrinsic value and the time value.
- The *gearing effect* of warrants refers to the possibility of making higher percentage gains by buying warrants than by buying the underlying share.

For example, if $N = 5$, $P = £1.25$ and $E = £1$, then the intrinsic value $V_w = 0.25 \times 5 = £1.25$. If, over time, the share price rises from £1.25 to £2.50, the intrinsic value V_w increases to:

$$V_w = (2.50 - 1.00) \times 5 = £7.50$$

The value of the underlying ordinary share increases by 100%, but the value of the warrant increases by 500%. A greater proportional gain results from buying the warrant than from buying the ordinary share.

For investors, the attractions of buying warrants rather than shares include:

- lower initial outlay;
- higher relative profit potential due to the gearing effect of warrants;
- lower relative loss potential.

For companies, the use of warrants may be attractive because:

- the interest rate on sweetened bonds will be lower than that on similar ordinary bonds;
- attaching warrants will make a bond issue more attractive to investors.

The valuation of fixed-interest bonds

Irredeemable bonds

The ex-interest market value of an irredeemable bond is the sum to infinity of the discounted future interest payments, as follows:

$$P_0 = \frac{I}{K_d}$$

where: P_0 = ex-interest market value (£)
I = annual interest paid (£)
K_d = rate of return required by debt investors, i.e. the cost of debt (%).

For example, if I = £10 per year and K_d = 9.1%, P_0 = 10/0.091 = £109.89.

■ Redeemable bonds

The ex-interest market value of a redeemable bond is the sum of the present values of the future interest payments and the future redemption value, discounted by the debt holders' required rate of return:

$$P_0 = \frac{I}{(1+K_d)} + \frac{I}{(1+K_d)^2} + \frac{I}{(1+K_d)^3} + \cdots + \frac{I+RV}{(1+K_d)^n}$$

where: P_0 = ex-interest market value
I = interest paid (£)
K_d = rate of return required by debt investors or cost of debt (%)
RV = redemption value (£)
n = time to maturity (years).

For example, if I = £10 per year, K_d = 9% per year, n = 5 years and RV = £100, then the ex-interest market value P_0 = (10 × 3.890) + (100 × 0.650) = £103.90.

The valuation of convertible bonds

Convertible bonds can be valued as ordinary bonds if conversion appears unlikely; their minimum price or floor value will therefore be the sum of the present values of the future interest payments and the principal repaid on maturity. Alternatively, if conversion appears likely, the market value of convertible bonds will be the sum of the present values of the future interest payments up to the conversion date and the present value of the conversion value.

■ Conversion value

The conversion value depends on the estimated share price on the conversion date, as follows:

$$CV = P_0 (1 + g)^n R$$

where: CV = conversion value of the convertible bond (£)
P_0 = current ex-dividend ordinary share price (£)
g = expected annual growth rate of ordinary share price (%)
n = time to conversion (years)
R = number of shares received on conversion.

■ Market value

The market value of a convertible bond, where conversion is expected, will be the sum of the present values of the future interest payments and the present value of the bond's conversion value, as follows:

$$V_0 = \frac{I}{(1+K_d)} + \frac{I}{(1+K_d)^2} + \frac{I}{(1+K_d)^3} + \dots + \frac{I+CV}{(1+K_d)^n}$$

where: V_0 = ex-interest market value (£)
I = interest paid (£)
K_d = rate of return required by investors (%)
CV = conversion value of the convertible bond (£)
n = time to maturity (years).

This can also be expressed as:

$$V_0 = \sum_{i=1}^{i=n} \frac{I}{(1+K_d)^i} + \frac{P_0(1+g)^n R}{(1+K_d)^n}$$

For example, if P_0 = £2.66, g = 6% per year, R = 30, I = £10 per year, K_d = 9% per year and n = 5 years, then:

conversion value after five years = 2.66 × 1.06^5 × 30
= £106.79;
ex-interest market value P_0 = (10 × 3.890) + (106.79 × 0.650)
= £108.31.

■ Factors influencing the market value of a convertible bond

From the bond valuation formula, the factors influencing the market value of a convertible bond are as follows:

- amount and frequency of the annual interest payments;
- number of years to maturity;
- number of years to conversion;
- current ordinary share price;
- expected growth rate in ordinary share price;
- conversion ratio of the bond;
- the required return of the bondholders (the cost of debt).

Leasing

Leasing is short- to medium-term financing where an asset is leased by a lessee from a lessor. The lessee obtains the use of the leased asset while legal ownership remains with the lessor.

■ Forms of leasing

Statement of Standard Accounting Practice 21 distinguishes an operating lease from a finance lease.

Operating leases

Operating leases are essentially a rental agreement:

- the lessor tends to be responsible for servicing and maintenance;
- many different lessees use the leased asset during its useful economic life.

Under the accounting standard, only the lease rental obligations for the next accounting period are disclosed in the financial position statement: this is *off-balance-sheet financing*.

Finance leases

The accounting standard requires capitalisation of a finance lease in the financial position statement, since essentially the lessee owns the leased asset in everything but name. Under a finance lease:

- the lessee tends to be responsible for servicing and maintenance;
- the primary lease period is equal to the economic life of the leased asset;
- there is a primary and a secondary lease period;
- the secondary lease period is at a nominal rent.

■ Tax reasons for leasing

Leasing increased in popularity as a source of finance prior to 1984 for primarily tax-driven reasons, linked to low levels of corporate profitability. After 1984, changes to the tax system and accounting standards did not prevent the popularity of leasing from increasing further.

■ Non-tax reasons for leasing

Important reasons why leasing continues to be a popular source of finance include:

- leasing provides a source of finance even if a company is short of liquidity;
- leasing provides a source of finance even if a company is short of security to support borrowing, as the leased asset can be reclaimed in the event of default on lease rentals;
- leasing offers a solution to the obsolescence problem;
- operating leases remain off balance sheet;
- lease contracts are flexible as regards choice of equipment and lease payment scheduling.

■ Evaluating leasing as a source of finance

In order to avoid suboptimal investment decisions, the financing choice should be made first, in which case the financing decision is separate from the investment decision. The financing choice can be evaluated by comparing leasing with borrowing to buy on a discounted cash flow basis. Relevant cash flows in this evaluation include:

- tax benefits on capital allowances and lease payments, possibly taken one year in arrears;
- tax benefits on any balancing allowances or charges;
- maintenance costs and their associated tax benefits, if paid by one party and not the other;
- lease payments, paying careful attention to their amount and timing;
- the purchase price and disposal value of the asset in question.

The discount rate to use is the before- or after-tax cost of borrowing of the company.

Example

Evaluation of leasing versus borrowing to buy

Given the following information, is leasing or buying preferred?

Life of machine:	6 years
Cost of machine:	£90 000
Lease rentals:	£20 000 per year, payable at the start of each year
Maintenance costs:	£1000 per year if machine is bought
Profit tax:	30% per year one year in arrears
Capital allowances:	25% per year reducing balance basis
Cost of borrowing:	10% per year before tax

Suggested answer

After-tax cost of borrowing = $10 \times (1 - 0.30) = 7\%$.

Table 5.1 Present cost of leasing

Years	Cash flow	(£)	7% discount factors	Present value (£)
0–5	Lease payments	(20 000)	(4.100 + 1.000) = 5.100	(102 000)
2–7	Tax relief	6 000	(5.389 – 0.935) = 4.454	26 724
				(75 276)

Table 5.2 Tax benefit calculation if buying is used

Year	Capital allowances (£)	Operating costs (£)	Total (£)	30% tax relief (£)	Taken in year
1	22 500	1000	23 500	7050	2
2	16 875	1000	17 875	5363	3
3	12 656	1000	13 656	4097	4
4	9 492	1000	10 492	3148	5
5	7 119	1000	8 119	2436	6
6	21 358	1000	22 358	6707	7

Table 5.3 Present cost of borrowing to buy

Year	Capital (£)	Operating costs (£)	Tax relief (£)	Net cash flow (£)	7% discount factors	Present value (£)
0	(90 000)			(90 000)	1.000	(90 000)
1		(1 000)		(1 000)	0.935	(935)
2		(1 000)	7050	6050	0.873	5282
3		(1 000)	5363	4363	0.816	3560
4		(1 000)	4097	3097	0.763	2363
5		(1 000)	3148	2148	0.713	1532
6		(1 000)	2436	1436	0.666	956
7			6707	6707	0.623	4179
						(73 063)

Buying is recommended as the cost of leasing (£75 276) is slightly higher than the cost of borrowing (£73 063).

▌ Distribution of financial benefits

Leasing must be beneficial to both lessor and lessee. Tax benefits may arise if either party is faced with different cash flows as a result of:

- different costs of capital;
- different tax rates;
- different abilities to benefit from capital allowances.

The distribution of financial benefits depends on the size and timing of lease payments.

Evaluating the financial effect of financing choices

Evaluating the financial effect of a financing choice helps a company to make the best choice:

- changes in shareholder wealth can be found by calculating the effect of a financing choice on the share price, using the price/earnings ratio method and the new earnings per share;
- changes in financial risk can be examined by calculating the effect of a financing choice on gearing and on the interest coverage ratio, referenced perhaps to suitable benchmarks.

(These evaluations are tricky: study carefully the example on pp. 150–1 in the textbook.)

Examination pointers

✔ A thorough understanding of debt is needed when answering financing questions, so study with care the various features of debt finance, such as tax efficiency, restrictive covenants, redemption, security, interest income versus capital gains, and variable interest rates.

✔ Make sure you understand the cash flows associated with convertible bonds, and the way that the choice between conversion and redemption affect their valuation.

✔ A good understanding of the attractions of convertible debt as a source of finance means that you are likely to be able to discuss the attractions of most kinds of debt.

✔ Check that you can calculate the market value of any bond you might meet in an exam.

✔ Warrants might be unlikely to appear in an exam, but the option concepts they illustrate could well be important.

✔ Leasing is a popular examination topic, in terms of both discussion and evaluation.

✔ Being able to evaluate the effect of different financing choices is a key skill in any corporate finance exam. It needs to be practised if it is to be applied well.

6

An overview of investment appraisal methods

Introduction

Capital investment:

- allows companies to generate cash flows in the future;
- enables companies to maintain the profitability of existing business activities;
- may require the investment of very large amounts of cash;
- needs to be evaluated appropriately in order to maximise the return to shareholders.

The payback method

This investment appraisal method calculates the number of years needed to recover the original investment and the *decision rule* is to accept a project if the payback period is equal to or less than a stated target value.

Example of the payback method

Consider an investment project with the following cash flows:

Year	0	1	2	3	4	5
Cash flow (£)	(450)	100	200	100	100	80

After three years, £400 will be recovered and £50 will be outstanding at the start of the fourth year. Therefore the payback period = 3 + (50/100) = 3.5 years.

■ The advantages of the payback method

The advantages of the payback method include:

- it is simple and easy to apply and straightforward to understand;
- it uses cash flows, not accounting profits;
- it takes account of risk, if risk is related to uncertainty.

■ The disadvantages of the payback method

The disadvantages of the payback method include:

- it ignores the time value of money (although discounted payback can help here);
- it ignores all cash flows outside the payback period;
- the choice of the target payback period is arbitrary.

The payback method does not give any real indication of project acceptability and, rather than being an investment appraisal method, it is really a way of assessing the effect of an investment project on a company's liquidity.

The return on capital employed method

The return on capital employed (ROCE) – also called the return on investment or the accounting rate of return – relate accounting profit to the capital invested. One widely used definition is:

$$\text{ROCE} = \frac{\text{Average annual accounting profit}}{\text{Average investment}} \times 100$$

Average investment takes account of any scrap value, as follows:

$$\text{Average investment} = \frac{\text{Initial investment} + \text{Scrap value}}{2}$$

Another common definition of ROCE uses the initial investment:

$$ROCE = \frac{\text{Average annual accounting profit}}{\text{Initial (or final) investment}} \times 100$$

Accounting profits are before-tax operating cash flows adjusted to take account of depreciation and hence are not cash flows. The *decision rule* is to accept investments with a ROCE greater than a target rate of return. If two investment projects are mutually exclusive, the project with the higher ROCE is accepted.

Example

Calculating ROCE

Given the following information, is the investment acceptable?

Initial cost: £570 000   Net cash receipts: £210 000 per year
Scrap value: £70 000   Investment life: 5 years
Target ROCE using average investment method: 20%

Suggested answer   £

Total cash profit = 210 000 × 5 =	1 050 000
Total depreciation = 570 000 − 70 000 =	500 000
Total accounting profit	550 000
Average annual accounting profit = 550 000/5 =	£110 000 per year
Average investment = (570 000 + 70 000)/2 =	£320 000
Return on capital employed = 100 × (110 000/320 000) =	34.4%

The investment has a ROCE greater than the target value and is therefore acceptable.

■ Advantages of the return on capital employed method

The advantages of ROCE include:

- it gives a value in percentage terms, which is a familiar measure of return;
- it is relatively simple method to apply compared to NPV or IRR;
- it can be used to compare mutually exclusive projects;
- it considers all cash flows arising during the life of a project.

■ Disadvantages of the return on capital employed method

Disadvantages of ROCE as an investment appraisal method include:

- it uses accounting profit, rather than cash;
- it uses average profits and so ignores the timing of profits;
- it does not consider the time value of money;
- it is expressed in percentage terms and hence is a relative measure of project worth.

For these reasons, ROCE does not really offer advice as to whether a project creates wealth.

The net present value (NPV) method

The NPV method compares the sum of the present values of all future project cash flows with the initial capital invested. A positive NPV indicates that an investment project gives a return in excess of the discount rate or cost of capital and will therefore increase shareholder wealth. The decision rule is to accept all projects with a positive NPV. If two investment projects are mutually exclusive, the project with the higher NPV is selected. NPV can be represented as:

$$\text{NPV} = I_0 + \frac{C_1}{(1+r)} + \frac{C_2}{(1+r)^2} + \frac{C_3}{(1+r)^3} + \cdots + \frac{C_n}{(1+r)^n}$$

where: I_0 = the initial investment

$C_1, C_2, ..., C_n$ = the project cash flows occurring in years $1, 2, ..., n$

r = the cost of capital or required rate of return.

Cash flows occurring during a time period are assumed to occur at the end of that period.

Example

Calculating the NPV an investment project

Given the following information, calculate whether the project is acceptable using the NPV method and a discount rate of 10%.

Year	0	1	2	3	4	5
Cash flow (£)	(4000)	800	900	1200	1400	1600

Suggested answer

Year	0	1	2	3	4	5
Cash flow (£)	(4000)	800	900	1200	1400	1600
Discount at 10%	1.000	0.909	0.826	0.751	0.683	0.621
Present values (£)	(4000)	727	743	901	956	994

NPV = 4321 − 4000 = £321

As the NPV is positive, the project is acceptable.

■ Advantages of the NPV method

The NPV method of investment appraisal has several advantages:

■ it takes account of the time value of money;
■ it uses cash flows rather than accounting profit;
■ it is an absolute measure of the value of an investment project;
■ it takes account of all relevant cash flows over the life of an investment project.

For all these reasons, NPV is the academically preferred method of investment appraisal. In all cases where capital is not rationed, the NPV decision rule offers sound investment advice.

■ Disadvantages of the NPV method

One criticism of the NPV decision rule is that it is only possible to accept all projects with a positive NPV in a perfect capital market. In reality, capital is rationed and this can limit the applicability of the NPV decision rule.

The internal rate of return (IRR) method

The IRR of an investment project is the cost of capital which gives an NPV of zero and an investment project is acceptable if the IRR is greater than the company's cost of capital. If comparing two projects, the one with the higher IRR is preferred.

Example

Calculating the IRR of an investment project

Given the following information, calculate whether the project is acceptable using the IRR method. The cost of capital of the investing company is 10%.

Year	0	1	2	3	4	5
Cash flow (£)	(4000)	800	900	1200	1400	1600

Suggested answer

NPV at 10% = £321 (see previous example)

Year	0	1	2	3	4	5
Cash flow (£)	(4000)	800	900	1200	1400	1600
Discount at 20%	1.000	0.833	0.694	0.579	0.482	0.402
Present values (£)	(4000)	666	625	695	675	643

NPV at 20% = 3304 − 4000 = (£696)

Using linear interpolation,

IRR = 10 + [(20 − 10) × 321]/(321 + 696) = 10 + 3.2 = 13.2%

This is only a first approximation of the IRR and selecting different discount rates would give a different value for IRR. *Note that linear interpolation is explained in detail in the textbook.*

As the IRR is greater than the cost of capital of 10%, the project is acceptable.

(A comprehensive example of IRR calculations can be found on pp.170–3 in the textbook.)

■ Advantages of the IRR method

The IRR method of investment appraisal has several advantages:

- ■ it takes account of the time value of money;
- ■ it uses cash flows rather than accounting profit;
- ■ it gives a measure of investment worth, which is comparable to economic variables such as interest rates and inflation rates;
- ■ the difference between the IRR and the cost of capital can be seen as a margin of safety;
- ■ it takes account of all relevant cash flows over the life of an investment project.

A comparison of the NPV and IRR methods

There is no conflict between NPV and IRR when evaluating a single investment project with conventional cash flows. NPV always offers the correct advice in the following situations:

- ■ where mutually exclusive projects are being compared;
- ■ where the cash flows of a project are non-conventional;
- ■ where the discount rate changes during the life of the project.

∎ Mutually exclusive projects

With mutually exclusive projects, IRR may offer investment advice which conflicts with that offered by NPV. Whenever this conflict occurs, the correct decision is to choose the project with the higher NPV, as this decision leads to the greatest increase in shareholder wealth.

∎ Non-conventional cash flows

If investment project cash flows change sign in successive periods (e.g. a cash inflow followed by a cash outflow), the investment project may have more than one IRR. Such cash flows are called non-conventional cash flows. Multiple IRR values may lead to incorrect decisions being taken if the IRR decision rule is applied. The NPV method always offers the correct investment advice with non-conventional cash flows.

∎ Changes in the discount rate

If there are changes in the cost of capital during an investment project, the NPV method can easily accommodate them. If the discount rates in successive years are r_1, r_2, etc., we have:

$$NPV = I_0 + \frac{C_1}{(1+r_1)} + \frac{C_2}{(1+r_1)(1+r_2)}$$

∎ Reinvestment assumptions

The NPV method assumes that project cash flows can be reinvested at the cost of capital, while the IRR method assumes that project cash flows can be reinvested at the IRR, which is not a rate found in the real world. The reinvestment assumption underlying the IRR method is therefore unrealistic compared to the reinvestment assumption underlying the NPV method.

■ The superiority of the NPV method

NPV is preferred to IRR because NPV:

- ■ gives correct advice about mutually exclusive projects;
- ■ can take account of non-conventional cash flows;
- ■ has a realistic assumption;
- ■ can easily incorporate changes in the discount rate.

The profitability index and capital rationing

Capital rationing occurs when a company has insufficient funds to undertake all projects with a positive NPV. In this imperfect capital market, ranking investment projects by absolute NPV may not lead to correct investment decisions, since a combination of smaller projects may lead to a higher NPV. Instead, investment projects can be ranked with the profitability index.

■ Hard capital rationing

Reasons for hard (externally imposed) capital rationing include:

- ■ capital markets are depressed;
- ■ investors consider the company to be too risky;
- ■ issue costs may make raising small amounts of finance expensive.

■ Soft capital rationing

Soft (internally imposed) capital rationing may arise because managers:

- ■ decide not to issue more equity in order to avoid dilution of control or earnings per share;
- ■ decide not to raise debt finance in order to avoid fixed interest payment obligations;
- ■ limit the investment funds available due to a preference for steady growth;
- ■ create a competitive internal market for available investment funds.

■ Single-period capital rationing

If funds are restricted in the first period (i.e. in year 0), the combination of projects that maximises NPV can be found by ranking via the profitability index or by evaluating combinations of projects.

Divisible, non-deferrable investment projects

If investment projects are divisible, non-deferrable and non-repeatable and if capital is rationed in the initial period alone, projects can be *ranked* by the profitability index:

$$\text{Profitability index} = \frac{\text{Present value of future cash flows}}{\text{Value of initial capital invested}}$$

Funds are then invested in projects according to the ranking until insufficient funds remain for the next project; remaining funds are then invested pro rata in that project. The total NPV is the sum of the NPV of the complete projects, plus the pro rata share of the NPV of the part project, as shown in Table 6.1. The profitability index can also be defined as the ratio of NPV to initial capital invested.

Indivisible, non-deferrable investment projects

If investment projects are not divisible, the combination with the highest NPV which does not exceed the available investment capital is optimal.

■ Multiple-period capital rationing

If investment funds are restricted in more than one period, the investment decision can be solved using linear programming.

Table 6.1 Total net present value

Project	A	B	C	D
Initial investment (£)	500	650	800	850
Net present value (£)	650	715	800	765
PV of future cash flows (£)	1150	1365	1600	1615
Profitability index	2.3	2.1	2.0	1.9
Ranking by NPV	4	3	1	2
Ranking by profitability index	1	2	3	4

Capital available = £1650		
Optimum investment schedule:	NPV (£)	Cumulative investment (£)
£500 invested in Project A	650	500
£650 invested in Project B	715	1150
£500 invested in Project C	500	1650
Total NPV for £1650 invested:	1865	

The discounted payback method

The payback method can be used with discounted cash flows to take account of the time value of money. This removes one of the disadvantages of this investment appraisal method.

Examination pointers

✔ Make sure you understand the relative advantages and disadvantages of the four main investment appraisal methods: return on capital employed (ROCE), payback, net present value (NPV) and internal rate of return (IRR).

✔ Practise applying these investment appraisal methods so that, in an examination situation, you can carry out the assessment requirement quickly and accurately.

✔ Calculating IRR is a technique that is also needed in calculating the cost of debt, so it pays to master this skill.

✔ Be ready to explain why NPV is regarded as superior to IRR.

✔ Capital rationing is often examined, so remember the difference between the hard and soft versions, and be prepared to calculate an investment plan that maximises NPV using the profitability index.

7

Investment appraisal: applications and risk

Introduction

If investment appraisal methods are applied to real world decisions, we may need to consider:

- the effects of taxation and inflation;
- the effects of risk and uncertainty;
- the evaluation of foreign direct investment;
- how investment proposals are appraised in practice.

Relevant project cash flows

Investment appraisal should include only relevant cash flows, which are cash flows that change as a result of an investment decision, i.e. incremental cash flows.

Sunk costs

These are costs incurred before an investment project begins, for example market research. Sunk costs are not relevant costs, since they will be paid regardless of whether a project is undertaken.

■ Apportioned fixed costs

These costs – for example, apportioned rent – are not relevant as they are not incremental costs.

■ Opportunity costs

This cost is the benefit given up by using an asset for one purpose rather than another.

■ Incremental working capital

An increase in net working capital (inventory plus receivables less payables) that arises due to an investment project is a relevant cost, as is incremental investment in working capital as sales levels increase. If an investment project ends, the investment in working capital will be recovered.

Taxation and capital investment decisions

Corporate tax benefits and liabilities must be considered in an investment appraisal.

■ Capital allowances

The government allows capital expenditure to be written off against taxable profits by means of annual capital allowances or tax-allowable depreciation. In the UK the standard capital allowance on plant and machinery is 20% on a reducing balance basis. A balancing allowance or balancing charge will equate total capital allowances to the value consumed by the business (capital cost minus scrap value). The current (2009) UK corporation tax rate ranges from 21% to 28%.

An example of calculating capital allowances on plant and machinery on a 20% reducing balance basis, with associated tax benefits at a rate of 28%, is given opposite.

	Capital allowances		Tax benefits
	£	£	£
Year 1: 200 000 × 0.2 =		40 000	11 200
Year 2: (200 000 − 40 000) × 0.2 =		32 000	8 960
Year 3: (200 000 − 40 000 − 32 000) × 0.2 =		25 600	7 168
Year 4: (200 000 − 40 000 − 32 000 − 25 600) × 0.2 =		20 480	
Initial value =	200 000		
Scrap value =	20 000		
Value consumed by the business over 4 years =	180 000		
Sum of capital allowances to end of Year 4 =	118 080		
Year 4 balancing allowance =		61 920	23 072
Total capital allowances over 4 years =		180 000	50 400

∎ Tax allowable costs

Tax liability is reduced by deducting tax-allowable costs, such as wages and salaries, when calculating taxable profit.

∎ Are interest payments a relevant cash flow?

Interest payments on debt must not be included in a domestic investment appraisal because the cost of capital used as the discount rate includes the effect of interest payments. The tax shield on debt is accounted for by using an after-tax discount rate.

■ The timing of tax liabilities and benefits

Tax benefits and liabilities can be taken in the year that taxable profit arises, or in the next year, depending on the situation in the real world. The method used in the textbook to account for the tax effects of capital allowances and reduce errors in calculation is:

- capital investment occurs at Year 0;
- the first capital allowance affects cash flows arising in Year 1;
- the benefit from the first capital allowance arises in Year 2;
- the number of capital allowances is equal to the number of years in the life of the project.

■ Can taxation be ignored?

The financial acceptability of an investment project can be affected by taxation when taxable profit is different from project cash flow and when inflation is included in project evaluation.

Inflation and capital investment decisions

Investment appraisal can take account of inflation in two ways:

- by discounting nominal (money) cash flows with a nominal cost of capital;
- by discounting real cash flows with a real cost of capital.

■ Real and nominal costs of capital

The real cost of capital is found by deflating the nominal (or money) cost of capital.

$$(1 + \text{Nominal cost of capital}) =$$
$$(1 + \text{Real cost of capital}) \times (1 + \text{Inflation rate})$$

This relationship, the Fisher equation, can be rearranged to give:

$$(1 + \text{Real cost of capital}) = \frac{(1 + \text{Nominal cost of capital})}{(1 + \text{Inflation rate})}$$

Deflating a nominal cost of capital of 15% by an inflation rate of 9% gives a real cost of capital of 5.5%:

$$(1 + 0.15)/(I + 0.09) = 1.055$$

∎ General and specific inflation

General inflation represents an average increase in prices, for example, as measured by the consumer price index (CPI). Specific inflation refers to how individual costs and prices inflate at different rates. The general rate of inflation can be used:

- to deflate a nominal cost of capital to a real cost of capital;
- to deflate nominal cash flows to real cash flows.

∎ Inflation and working capital

The real value of working capital is maintained by incremental investment which increases its nominal value. If an investment project ends, the nominal value of working capital invested is recovered.

∎ The golden rule for dealing with inflation in investment appraisal

The golden rule is to discount real cash flows with a real cost of capital and to discount nominal cash flows with a nominal cost of capital. The NPV given by the real terms approach is the same as the NPV given by the nominal terms approach.

Example

NPV calculation involving inflation

A comprehensive worked example can be found on pp. 197–8 in the textbook.

Investment appraisal: risk and uncertainty

Risk, in the context of investment appraisal:

- refers to circumstances to which probabilities can be assigned;
- refers to business risk, as financial risk is accommodated by the project discount rate;
- increases with the variability of returns.

Uncertainty, in the context of investment appraisal:

- implies that circumstances cannot be quantified;
- increases with project life.

The distinction between risk and uncertainty has little significance in real business decisions.

Sensitivity analysis

Sensitivity analysis evaluates how changes in project variables affect the NPV of a project. There are two methods:

- finding the relative change needed in a project variable to make the NPV zero;
- finding the relative change in the NPV for a fixed change in a project variable.

Both methods indicate the key variables, i.e. those where a relatively small change can have a significant adverse effect on NPV, and these variables can be investigated further.

Problems with sensitivity analysis include:

- it does not assess project risk, as it does not assess the probability of changes in project variables;
- only one variable at a time can be changed, but project variables are not independent.

Example

Application of sensitivity analysis

Assess the sensitivity of the project to changes in initial investment, selling price and sales volume:

Initial investment: £7m
Selling price: £9.20 per unit
Sales volume: 800 000 units

Project life: 4 years
Cost: £6.00 per unit
Cost of capital: 12%

Suggested answer

	£
Present value of sales revenue =	
9.20 × 800 000 × 3.037 =	22 352 320
Present value of variable costs =	
6.00 × 800 000 × 3.037 =	14 577 600
Present value of contribution	7 774 720
Initial investment	7 000 000
Net present value	774 720

Initial investment

If the initial investment increases by £774 720, the NPV becomes zero:

$$100 \times (774\ 720/7\ 000\ 000) = 11.1\%$$

Sales price

The relative decrease in selling price per unit that makes the NPV zero is the ratio of the NPV to the present value of sales revenue:

$$100 \times (774\ 720/22\ 352\ 320) = 3.5\%$$

Sales volume

The relative decrease in sales volume that makes the NPV zero is the ratio of the NPV to the present value of contribution:

$$100 \times (774\ 720/7\ 774\ 720) = 10.0\%$$

■ Payback

Payback focuses on the near future and promotes short-term projects over those of longer term (and therefore maybe riskier). Risk can be included in investment appraisal by shortening the payback period for riskier projects. Payback has such serious problems as an investment appraisal method, however, that using it as a method of adjusting for risk is not recommended.

■ Conservative forecasts

This traditional way of dealing with risk in investment appraisal reduces future cash flows to more conservative values and then discounts these conservative cash flows by a risk-free rate of return. Problems with this method include:

■ cash flow reductions are subjective and may vary between projects;
■ cash flow reductions may be anticipated and forecasted cash flows increased to compensate;
■ attractive investments may be rejected due to the focus on conservative cash flows.

■ Risk-adjusted discount rates

Investors need a risk premium in addition to the risk-free rate of return, and the greater the risk of an investment, the greater the risk premium required. The risk premium for a specific investment is not easy to determine, however.

One solution is to assign investment projects to particular risk classes and discount them using the discount rate chosen for that class. This solution has several problems:

■ assessing the risk of a project;
■ choosing the discount rate for a risk class;
■ assuming that risk increases at a constant rate as the life of the project increases.

■ Probability analysis and expected net present value

A probability distribution of expected cash flows can be used to calculate:

- the average NPV, i.e. the expected net present value (ENPV);
- the probability of the worst case;
- the probability of failing to achieve a positive NPV.

This approach can give more useful information than single-point NPV estimates, but the ENPV is an average value that is not expected to occur in reality.

Example

Calculation of expected net present value

What is the ENPV of the following project?

Forecast	Probability	Net present value
Best case	0.2	€30 000
Most likely	0.7	€20 000
Worst case	0.1	€10 000

Suggested answer
ENPV = (0.2 × €30 000) + (0.7 × €20 000) + (0.1 × €10 000)
= €21 000

■ Simulation models

Simulation models calculate ENPV through repeated analysis based on probability distributions for each project variable and can accommodate simultaneous changes in these variables. The calculation process is described in the textbook. Managers can then make investment decisions based on:

- the return of the investment (its ENPV);
- the risk of the investment (the standard deviation of the ENPV).

Appraisal of foreign direct investment

Foreign direct investment (FDI) is a long-term investment, such as setting up a foreign subsidiary.

The distinctive features of foreign direct investment

FDI decisions are more difficult to evaluate than domestic investment decisions because:

- foreign currency project cash flows will need to be evaluated;
- foreign taxation systems may differ from the domestic taxation system;
- project cash flows and parent cash flows will be different;
- remittance of project cash flows may be restricted.

Methods of evaluating foreign direct investment

FDI proposals should be evaluated using the NPV method from a parent company perspective, since increasing the wealth of parent company shareholders is the primary financial objective. The relevant cash flows here are therefore the after-tax cash flows remitted to the parent company.

Evaluation of foreign direct investment at local level

FDI projects can be evaluated in local terms and in local currencies, using local project cash flows which include:

- *Initial investment* This will be investment in non-current assets, provided by debt or equity finance, as well as any transferred assets.
- *Investment in working capital* This may be part of the initial investment, or a transfer of inventory from the parent company.
- *Local after-tax cash flows* These cash flows will be sales revenue less local operating costs and local profit tax. Interest paid on locally raised debt must also be deducted. Transfer pricing may be an issue here.

■ *The terminal value of the project* A terminal value for the FDI project, such as an expected future market value, is used to limit the investment appraisal to a period over which cash flow forecasting is reasonably accurate.

■ Evaluation of foreign direct investment at parent company level

At parent company level, relevant project cash flows are the home currency cash receipts and payments, and any incremental changes in parent company cash flows.

■ *Initial investment* This is cash invested by the parent company and the opportunity cost of transferred assets.
■ *Returns on investment* The parent company may receive finance-related payments from the FDI project.
■ *Receipts from intercompany trade* The parent company may receive payment for goods and services provided to the FDI project.
■ *Taxation* Cash flows will be remitted after local taxation and will be liable for domestic tax.
■ *Exchange rates* Exchange rate forecasts for the life of the project will be needed, for example using purchasing power parity.
■ *Taxation and foreign direct investment* Double taxation relief means that the liability for domestic tax is reduced by the tax paid in the foreign country. The UK tax liability can be calculated from the foreign currency taxable profits of the foreign subsidiary and this liability can then be reduced by any tax already paid.

Example

Calculation of UK tax liability

Net cash flow of $2 190 000 is expected by a foreign subsidiary. Tax is paid at 20% in the foreign country and 28% in the UK. If all after-tax cash flows are remitted to the parent company and £1.00 = $2.63, what is the UK tax liability on the remittance?

Suggested answer
Year 1 taxable profit (£) = 2 190 000/2.63 = 832 700
UK tax liability = 832 700 × 0.28 = £233 156
Local tax paid = 832 700 × 0.20 = £166 540
UK tax liability = 233 156 – 166 540 = £66 616

(A comprehensive worked FDI example can be found on pp. 209–11 in the textbook.)

Empirical investigations of investment appraisal

In general, empirical findings are as follows:

- Discounted cash flow methods now appear to be more popular than non-DCF methods.
- Payback is used in large organisations in conjunction with other investment appraisal methods.
- IRR is more popular than NPV in small companies, but NPV is now the most popular investment appraisal method in large companies.
- ROCE, the least popular investment appraisal method, continues to be used with other methods.
- Companies tend not to use sophisticated methods to account for project risk.
- Sensitivity analysis is most often used to account for risk.
- Most companies allow for inflation using a theoretically correct method.
- Almost all companies use sensitivity analysis, an increasing minority of companies use probability analysis, very few companies use the capital asset pricing model.

■ Foreign direct investment

Empirical evidence suggests that many multinational companies (MNCs) use a range of methods to evaluate FDI decisions. The evidence indicates that:

■ most MNCs use DCF methods, with IRR being preferred to NPV;
■ many companies do not use after-tax parent cash flows as the main income measure;
■ some MNCs appear to base the FDI discount rate on the cost of debt;
■ smaller firms tend to use non-DCF methods such as ROCE and payback.

■ Conclusions of empirical investigations

The evidence indicates that:

■ most companies use a combination of investment appraisal methods;
■ there are differences between the methods used by small and large companies;
■ most companies now deal with inflation correctly.

Examination pointers

✔ Mistakes are often made when selecting relevant cash flows in investment appraisal questions, so check your understanding of this crucial topic.

✔ Many students experience difficulty when incorporating taxation and inflation into investment appraisal, so it is essential to practise answering questions in this area in order to improve your examination technique. Investment appraisal questions often carry high marks!

✔ Make sure you understand the difference between risk and uncertainty!

✔ Sensitivity analysis and probability analysis are examined regularly, and are straightforward investment appraisal topics to master.

✔ Foreign direct investment exam questions usually carry high marks but a thorough knowledge of all areas of investment appraisal is needed to answer these questions well. The calculations, though somewhat complex, are repetitive and good technique is rewarded. The area that most students find hardest to master is calculating the UK tax liability.

8

Portfolio theory and the capital asset pricing model

Introduction

Portfolio theory and the capital asset pricing model look at key corporate finance concepts:

- rational investors seek to maximise return while minimising risk;
- risk can be measured by the variability of returns;
- portfolio theory shows how to reduce the level of risk faced by investors;
- the capital asset pricing model relates the required return to the level of systematic risk.

The measurement of risk

Risk can be measured by the standard deviation of historical or expected future returns.

Calculating risk and return using probabilities

The mean returns and standard deviations of the expected future returns of two shares are given by the following formulae:

Mean return of a share $\overline{R} = \sum_{i=1}^{n} P_i \times R_i$

Standard deviation (σ) = $\sqrt{\sum_{i=1}^{n} P_i \times (R_i - \overline{R})^2}$

where: $P_1, ..., P_n$ = the probabilities of the n different outcomes

$R_1, ..., R_n$ = the corresponding returns associated with the n different outcomes.

■ Calculating risk and return using historical data

The mean returns and standard deviations of the historical returns of two shares are given by the following formulae:

Mean return $\overline{R} = \dfrac{\sum\limits_{i=1}^{n} R_i}{n}$

Standard deviation (σ) = $\sqrt{\dfrac{\sum\limits_{i=1}^{n} (R_i - \overline{R})^2}{n}}$

(See pp. 225–8 in the textbook for worked examples of calculating risk and return.)

The concept of diversification

The total risk faced by investors and companies can be divided into:

■ *systematic risk*, which represents how returns on a share are affected by systematic factors such as changes in interest rates (also called non-diversifiable or market risk);

■ *unsystematic risk*, which is the risk specific to a particular share, i.e. the risk of a company performing badly or going into liquidation (also called diversifiable or specific risk).

◼ Diversifying unsystematic risk: at a company or investor level?

Unsystematic risk can be diversified away at the company level (by diversifying business operations) and at the investor level (by holding a diversified portfolio of shares). Corporate diversification is less efficient than investor diversification because, at the corporate level:

- if business operations are scaled down, economies of scale can be lost;
- diversified companies may operate in business areas where they have less expertise;
- managing diversified companies is likely to be more complicated and more expensive.

The link between systematic risk, unsystematic risk and diversification is shown in Figure 8.1.

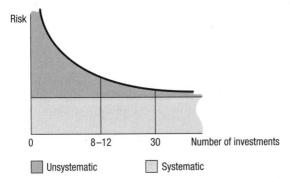

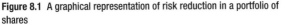

Figure 8.1 A graphical representation of risk reduction in a portfolio of shares

While corporate diversification at an international level reduces over-exposure to individual economies and cash flow volatility – and hence reduces business risk – it can also be argued that investors can diversify internationally. International diversification can reduce systematic risk.

■ Diversifying unsystematic risk using a two-share portfolio

Portfolio reduction of unsystematic risk depends on the extent to which returns on assets are correlated. This is measured by the correlation coefficient (ρ) of the returns of two shares, which can take any value in the range –1 to 1:

■ If $\rho_{x,y} = 1$, no unsystematic risk can be diversified away.
■ If $\rho_{x,y} = 0$, no correlation between the returns on share x and share y.
■ If $\rho_{x,y} = -1$, all unsystematic risk will be diversified away.

While maximum risk diversification occurs when $\rho_{x,y} = -1$, risk diversification occurs as long as $\rho_{x,y} < 1$. The correlation coefficient can be calculated by the formula:

$$\rho_{x,y} = \frac{Cov_{x,y}}{\sigma_x \, \sigma_y}$$

where $Cov_{x,y}$ is the covariance of returns of shares x and y.
For expected future returns, $\rho_{x,y}$ is given by:

$$\rho_{x,y} = \frac{\sum_{i=1}^{n} P_i \left(R_{ix} - \bar{R}_x\right) \times \left(R_{iy} - \bar{R}_y\right)}{\sigma_x \, \sigma_y}$$

For historical returns, $\rho_{x,y}$ is given by:

$$\rho_{x,y} = \frac{\sum_{i=1}^{n} P_i \left(R_{ix} - \bar{R}_x\right) \times \left(R_{iy} - \bar{R}_y\right)}{n\sigma_x \, \sigma_y}$$

The return of a two-share portfolio (R_p) is the weighted average of the two shares' returns:

$$R_p = (W_x R_x) + (W_y R_y)$$

The standard deviation (risk) of a two-share portfolio (σ_p) is given by:

$$\sigma_p = \sqrt{(W_x)^2 (\sigma_x)^2 + (W_y)^2 (\sigma_y)^2 + 2W_x W_y \sigma_x \sigma_y \rho_{x.y}}$$

where:

W_x = percentage of funds invested in share x
W_y = percentage of funds invested in share y
σ_x = standard deviation of share x's returns (%)
σ_y = standard deviation of share y's returns (%)
$\rho_{x.y}$ = correlation coefficient between x's and y's returns
σ_p = standard deviation of portfolio containing x and y (%).

(A numerical example of these calculations is found on pp. 231–2 in the textbook.)

The relationship between return and risk in a two-share portfolio is shown in Figure 8.2. From Figure 8.2, note that two-share portfolios B, C and D are preferred by investors because:

■ they offer a higher return for a given level of risk, or;
■ they offer a lower risk for a given level of return.

Introducing further shares into the portfolio increases the diversification of unsystematic risk and this principle forms the basis of Markowitz's portfolio theory.

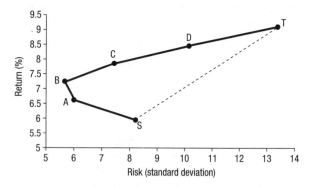

Figure 8.2 A graphical representation of return and risk in a two-share portfolio

Investor attitudes to risk

Investors have the following attitudes towards risk:

- risk-loving, where a high return is preferred in exchange for a high level of risk;
- risk-neutral, where there is indifference to the level of risk faced;
- risk-averse, where low-risk, low-return investments are preferred.

Utility curves (indifference curves) represent attitudes to different combinations of risk and return. Positive utility is gained from increasing return, while negative utility is gained from increasing risk. Rational investors will always try to increase their utility by seeking the highest return for a given level of risk, or by seeking the lowest risk for a given level of return. Utility curves differ in shape according to investor attitudes to risk and returns.

(Utility curves are explained in detail on pp. 232–5 in the textbook.)

Markowitz's portfolio theory

This theory (see Figure 8.3) rests on the ability of investors to diversify away unsystematic risk by holding diversified portfolios:

- The *envelope curve* is the set of all combinations of risky assets.
- Rational investors will chose portfolios on the *efficient frontier* as these portfolios give the highest return for a given level of risk or the lowest risk for a given level of return.
- If investors can lend and borrow at the risk-free rate of return, the *capital market line* can be constructed, linking the risk-free rate of return with the return on the *market portfolio.*
- The market portfolio represents the optimal combination of risky assets.
- The risk-free rate is usually approximated by the yield on Treasury bills.
- The capital market line represents a set of two-asset portfolios with a linear trade-off between total risk and return.

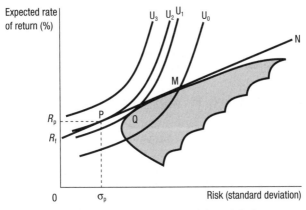

Figure 8.3 A graphical representation of Markowitz's portfolio theory

Investors will always choose capital market line portfolios as these are more efficient than those on the efficient frontier:

- Risk-averse investors will choose CML portfolios between R_f and M, putting their funds into the risk-free asset and the market portfolio; the optimal portfolio is the one tangential to the utility curve (point P).
- Risk-loving investors will choose portfolios on the CML between M and N by borrowing further funds at the risk-free rate and investing these in the market portfolio alone.

(Markovitz's portfolio theory is explained on pp. 235–7 in the textbook.)

■ Problems with the practical application of portfolio theory

There are practical problems in using portfolio theory, including:

- it is unrealistic to assume that investors can borrow at the risk-free rate;
- it is difficult to identify the market portfolio;
- it is difficult to construct the market portfolio due to transaction costs;
- the composition of the market portfolio changes over time.

Smaller investors can overcome this problem by investing in already diversified assets, such as index tracker funds.

Introduction to the capital asset pricing model

Portfolio theory considers total risk, while the capital asset pricing model (CAPM) considers systematic risk alone. The key assumptions of the CAPM are:

- investors are rational and want to maximise their utility;
- information is freely available to investors;
- investors can borrow and lend at the risk-free rate;

- investors hold diversified portfolios, eliminating all unsystematic risk;
- capital markets are perfect;
- investment occurs over a single, standardised holding period.

Using the CAPM to value shares

The linear relationship between risk and return in the CAPM (see Figure 8.4) is defined by the security market line (SML), which has the following equation:

$$R_j = R_f + \beta_j(R_m - R_f)$$

where: R_j = the rate of return of security j predicted by the model
R_f = the risk-free rate of return
β_j = the beta coefficient of security j
R_m = the return of the market.

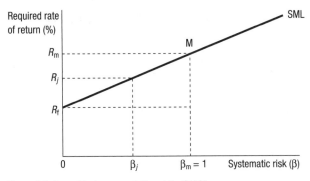

Figure 8.4 A graphical representation of the CAPM

■ The meaning and calculation of beta

The beta (β) of a share measures the sensitivity of the returns on the share to changes in the capital market, i.e. to changes in systematic factors:

- by definition, the beta of the market is 1;
- if the beta of a share is < 1, the share's systematic risk is less than that of the market;
- if the beta of a share is > 1, the share's systematic risk is more than that of the market.

Beta can be calculated from the following equation:

$$\beta_j = \frac{Cov_{j,m}}{(\sigma_m)^2} = \frac{\sigma_j \times \sigma_m \times \rho_{j,m}}{(\sigma_m)^2} = \frac{\sigma_j \times \rho_{j,m}}{\sigma_m}$$

where:

σ_j = standard deviation of returns of share j

σ_m = standard deviation of market returns

$\rho_{j,m}$ = correlation coefficient between share's returns and market returns

$Cov_{j,m}$ = covariance of returns of share j and the market.

- The most important determinant of a company's beta is the nature of its business.
- The portfolio beta is the market-value weighted average of betas of individual shares.

(Information on equity betas can be found on pp. 239–43 in the textbook.)

■ Determining the risk-free rate and the return of the market

The risk-free rate can be approximated by the yield on short-dated government bonds such as UK Treasury bills.

The return of the market can be approximated by using a stock exchange index such as the FTSE 100 as a representation of the market, together with the dividend yield of the market:

$$R_m = \frac{P_1 - P_0}{P_0} + \text{Div}$$

where: P_0 = the stock exchange index at the beginning of the period

P_1 = the stock exchange index at the end of the period

Div = average dividend yield of the stock exchange index over the period.

Short-term fluctuations in stock exchange indices make it advisable to use a time-smoothed average to estimate the return of the market.

Empirical studies have tried to quantify the market or equity risk premium $(R_m - R_f)$, which represents the excess of market returns over the returns from risk-free assets. Results vary considerably according to the time period used as a basis, whether a geometric or arithmetic average is calculated, and whether gilts or Treasury bills are used to represent the risk-free asset. While a market risk premium of between 8 and 9% has traditionally been quoted, a lower level of 5% has been suggested as a more appropriate current premium for equity risk.

■ A numerical example of the CAPM's use

If beta (β_j) = 1.17, the risk-free rate (R_f) = 3.1%, the market risk premium $(R_m - R_f)$ = 4.2%:

$$R_j = 3.1\% + (1.17 \times 4.2\%) = 8.0\%$$

■ Summary of the implications of the CAPM

■ The required rate of return of a share will be based on systematic risk, since diversification removes unsystematic risk.

■ Shares with higher levels of systematic risk should yield higher rates of return.

■ There should be a linear relationship between systematic risk and return, and shares that are priced correctly should plot on the security market line (SML).

Empirical tests of the CAPM

While the assumptions made by the CAPM do not mirror the real world, reality may not be so different from the assumptions as to invalidate the model. The CAPM should not be judged on its assumptions, therefore, but assessed on the results of its application.

Tests of the stability of beta

While the CAPM is a forward-looking model, betas are calculated using the historical returns of shares in relation to the historical returns of the market. The usefulness of the CAPM in pricing shares and appraising projects therefore depends heavily on the stability of beta over time:

■ empirical evidence on the stability of individual betas is inconclusive;

■ portfolio betas generally exhibit much higher stability over time than individual betas.

Tests of the security market line

Many empirical tests have compared a fitted SML derived by regression analysis with the theoretical SML, with the following conclusions:

■ The intercept of the fitted SML with the y-axis was above the intercept of the theoretical SML, indicating that factors other than systematic risk were influencing security returns.

■ The slope of the fitted SML was flatter than that of the theoretical SML.

■ The fitted SML indicated a strong linear relationship between systematic risk and return, although different from the one suggested by the theoretical SML.

In general, therefore, the CAPM does not fully explain observed data, even though systematic risk plays a significant role in explaining changes in the expected returns on shares. Recent research has not been supportive of the CAPM, although it may be argued that it is not possible to test the CAPM as it is not possible to create a perfect substitute for the market portfolio.

Reasons for retaining the CAPM, in spite of its limitations, include:

■ there is as yet no suitable replacement;
■ the CAPM gives a framework within which to analyse risk and return;
■ the CAPM is seen as superior to the dividend growth model for finding the cost of equity.

Examination pointers

✔ Many examination papers include a formula sheet, so work on *applying*, rather than memorising, the formulae relating to portfolio theory and the CAPM.

✔ Standard deviation is used to measure risk and the ability to calculate it is sometimes tested; the repetitive nature of the calculations involved should give easy marks.

✔ Understanding the meaning of the different risks in portfolio theory and the CAPM – systematic risk, unsystematic risk, business risk, financial risk – is an essential step in understanding the theories themselves.

✔ If you can explain the diagram illustrating Markowitz's portfolio theory (Figure 8.3) and all the lines and terms used in it, you are likely to do well in an examination question about this theory.

✔ The CAPM is of central importance in corporate finance theory and you must be able to explain all the key terms used in it, including market risk premium, equity beta, asset beta and security market line.

✔ You could be asked about the assumptions of the CAPM or about empirical research on the CAPM in an examination question about calculating the cost of equity or about investment appraisal, since the CAPM is used in both of these areas.

9

The cost of capital and capital structure

Introduction

Cost of capital and capital structure are closely related:

- a company's cost of capital can be used as the discount rate in investment appraisal;
- if the cost of capital is minimised, the value of a company is maximised;
- the minimum cost of capital corresponds to a company's optimal capital structure;
- there are arguments for and against the existence of an optimal capital structure.

Calculating the cost of individual sources of finance

The cost of capital of each source of *long-term* finance must be calculated before the weighted average cost of capital (WACC) can be calculated.

■ Ordinary shares

The dividend growth model can be rearranged to calculate the cost of equity (K_e):

$$K_e = \frac{D_0(1+g)}{P_0} + g$$

where: K_e = cost of equity
D_0 = current dividend or dividend to be paid shortly
g = expected annual growth rate in dividends
P_0 = ex-dividend share price.

Retained earnings are equity finance and have a cost of capital equal to the cost of equity.

The cost of equity can also be calculated using the capital asset pricing model (CAPM):

$$R_j = R_f + [\beta_j \times (R_m - R_f)]$$

where: R_j = the rate of return of share j predicted by the model
R_f = the risk-free rate of return
β_j = the beta coefficient of share j
R_m = the return of the market.

■ Preference shares

The cost of capital of irredeemable preference shares (K_{ps}) can be calculated as follows:

$$K_{ps} = \frac{\text{Dividend payable}}{\text{Market price (ex-dividend)}}$$

■ Bonds and convertibles

The before-tax cost of debt of irredeemable bonds (K_{ib}) can be calculated as follows:

$$K_{ib} = \frac{\text{Interest rate payable}}{\text{Market price of bond}}$$

The after-tax cost of debt of irredeemable bonds can be calculated as follows:

$$K_{ib} \text{ (after tax)} = K_{ib}(1 - C_T)$$

The after-tax cost of debt of redeemable bonds is the internal rate of return (K_d) of the bond valuation model:

$$P_0 = \frac{I(1-C_T)}{(1+K_d)} + \frac{I(1-C_T)}{(1+K_d)^2} + \frac{I(1-C_T)}{(1+K_d)^3} + ... + \frac{I(1-C_T)+RV}{(1+K_d)^n}$$

where: P_0 = current ex-interest market price of bond
I = annual interest payment
C_T = corporate taxation rate
RV = redemption value
K_d = after-tax cost of debt
n = number of years to redemption.

The value of K_d can be found by linear interpolation. The before-tax cost of debt of redeemable bonds can be calculated by using I and not $I(1 - C_T)$.

The before-tax cost of debt of redeemable bonds can also be calculated using the bond yield approximation model developed by Hawawini and Vora (1982):

$$K_d = \frac{I + \left[\dfrac{P - NPD}{n} \right]}{P + 0.6(NPD - P)}$$

where: I = annual interest payment
P = par value or face value
NPD = net proceeds from disposal (market price of bond)
n = number of years to redemption.

The after-tax cost of debt of redeemable bonds can then be calculated using:

$$K_d \text{ (after tax)} = K_d(1 - C_T)$$

The cost of debt of convertible bonds depends on expectations about conversion. If conversion is unlikely, the cost of debt can be calculated as for redeemable debt. If conversion is expected, the bond valuation is modified by replacing redemption value (RV) with conversion value (CV), and by replacing the number of years to redemption (n) with the number of years to conversion. The cost of debt of convertible bonds can then be found using linear interpolation.

■ Bank borrowings

An approximate before-tax cost of debt of bank borrowings is the interest paid on bank borrowings divided by the average amount of bank borrowings for the year. The cost of debt of redeemable bonds can be used as a substitute.

■ The relationship between the costs of different sources of finance

The cost of equity is the highest cost of capital as shareholders face the highest level of risk:

- dividend payments and capital gains are uncertain;
- equity finance is at the bottom of the creditor hierarchy if a company is liquidated.

The cost of preference shares is lower than the cost of equity because:

- preference dividends must be paid before ordinary dividends, so non-payment risk is lower;
- preference shares are above ordinary shares in the creditor hierarchy.

The cost of debt is lower than the cost of preference shares because:

- interest payments on debt are certain, unless bankruptcy is possible;
- debt is above preference shares and ordinary shares in the creditor hierarchy.

The ranking of the costs of debt of different sources of debt depend on:

- the relative issue costs;
- the amount of debt being raised;
- the period over which the debt is being raised;
- whether the debt is convertible or not;
- the extent and quality of security used.

Calculating the weighted average cost of capital

WACC is calculated by weighting the costs of the individual sources of finance:

$$\text{WACC} = \frac{K_e \times E}{(D+E)} + \frac{K_d(1-C_T) \times D}{(D+E)}$$

where: K_e = cost of equity
E = value of equity
K_d = before-tax cost of debt
C_T = corporate taxation rate
D = value of debt.

This equation uses only debt and equity, but can be expanded to include as many sources of finance as a company uses.

(Calculating the WACC is covered in detail on pp. 259–65 in the textbook.)

Market value weightings or book value weightings?

Book values (financial position statement values) are easy to obtain but should be avoided when calculating WACC because:

- book values are based on historical costs, whereas market values reflect the current return required by equity or debt investors;
- book values understate the impact of the cost of equity on the WACC and hence understate the WACC;
- if the WACC is understated, unprofitable projects will be accepted.

Average and marginal cost of capital

WACC can be calculated as the average cost of capital currently employed (which represents historical financial decisions) or as the cost of the next quantity of capital raised (which represents the marginal cost of capital). The relationship between average cost of capital (AC) and marginal cost of capital (MC) is as shown in Figure 9.1.

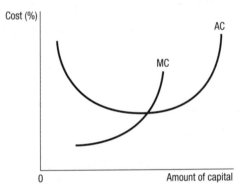

Figure 9.1 The relationship between average and marginal cost of capital

Although the marginal cost of capital, rather than the WACC, should theoretically be used in investment appraisal, an average cost of capital might be preferred because:

- it is often difficult to allocate particular funding to a specific project;
- companies with a target capital structure may raise marginal finance from different sources of finance over time, while maintaining the target capital structure on an average basis.

Using WACC as the discount rate in investment appraisal is appropriate if:

- the business risk of an investment project is similar to the business risk of the company's current activities (no change in business risk);
- incremental finance is raised in proportions which preserve the existing capital structure of the company (no change in financial risk);
- the incremental investment project does not disturb the risk/return relationships between existing providers of finance.

If these conditions are not satisfied, a marginal or project-specific cost of capital may be needed.

The CAPM and investment appraisal

The CAPM can be used to find a project-specific discount rate that reflects the systematic risk of an investment project.

Equity betas and asset betas

Systematic risk has two elements:

1 Business risk represents the sensitivity of corporate cash flows to changes in the economic climate within which a company operates.
2 Financial risk represents the sensitivity of corporate cash flows to changes in gearing and to changes in interest paid on its debt finance.

Equity beta systematic risk includes both business risk and financial risk. The asset beta is the weighted average of the equity beta and the debt beta, and includes only business risk:

$$\beta_a = \left[\beta_e \times \frac{E}{E + D(1 - C_T)} \right] + \left[\beta_d \times \frac{D(1 - C_T)}{E + D(1 - C_T)} \right]$$

where: β_a = asset beta
β_d = debt beta
β_e = equity beta
C_T = corporate tax rate
D = market value of debt
E = market value of equity.

If the debt beta is assumed to be zero, the equation becomes the *ungearing formula*:

$$\beta_a = \beta_e \times \frac{E}{E + D(1 - C_T)}$$

Rearranging this gives the *regearing formula*:

$$\beta_e = \beta_a \times \frac{E + D(1 - C_T)}{E}$$

■ Using the CAPM to calculate an investment project's discount rate

1 Find quoted companies with similar business operation to the investment project and take their equity betas as substitute (proxy) betas for the project beta.
2 Ungear the proxy equity betas to give proxy asset betas.
3 Calculate an average proxy asset beta and regear it to give an equity beta.
4 Use the CAPM and the regeared equity beta to calculate a project-specific cost of equity.

The project-specific cost of equity is an appropriate discount rate for a project financed by equity alone. If the project is financed by debt and equity, the project-specific cost of equity can be included in a project-specific WACC.

(A worked example is given on pp. 270–2 in the textbook, and this should be studied carefully.)

■ The benefits of using the CAPM instead of the WACC

Using the CAPM leads to better investment decisions in two areas (see Figure 9.2):

■ low-risk, low-return projects (A) – rejected using WACC – are accepted using the CAPM as their return compensates for their systematic risk;
■ high-risk, high-return projects (B) – accepted using WACC – are rejected using the CAPM as their return does not compensate for their systematic risk.

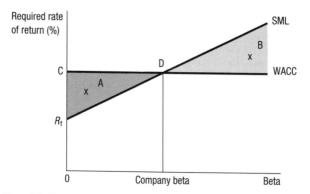

Figure 9.2 How the CAPM can lead to better investment decisions than the WACC

■ Problems using the CAPM in investment appraisal

There are many practical problems in using the CAPM in investment appraisal:

■ the CAPM's assumptions do not reflect the real world;
■ finding proxy equity betas can be difficult, as companies have diversified operations;

115

- it can be difficult to find information to ungear proxy equity betas;
- the CAPM uses a single period transaction horizon, but investment is over many periods;
- equity betas found using historical data may be unsuitable for making future decisions.

Practical problems with calculating WACC

Calculating the cost of sources of finance

- Market prices for traded bonds and shares may not be available.
- The cost of convertible bonds can be difficult to calculate.
- The cost of capital of leasing must be estimated.
- Interest payments may be covered by a swap agreement.
- The information used to calculate the cost of equity may be unreliable.

Which sources of finance should be included in the WACC?

- Finance funding long-term investment should be included in the WACC. Short-term debt should be excluded from the WACC unless it is being used to finance long-term assets.

Problems associated with weighting the sources

- Market values and book values are both used as weightings when calculating the WACC, since market values are not always available.

WACC is not constant

- WACC is not constant as the market values and cost of capital of each source of finance change over time.

The cost of capital for foreign direct investment

The cost of capital for foreign direct investment (FDI) should reflect systematic project risk, but there are difficulties in using the CAPM in FDI:

- Which market portfolio should be used in determining the project beta?
- Over what time frame should the cost of equity be determined?
- What is the value of the equity risk premium?

▌ The international financing decision

The objective of the international financing decision is to minimise the after-tax cost of capital at an acceptable level of risk, considering:

- relative proportions of equity and debt at parent and subsidiary level;
- relative proportions of long-term and short-term finance;
- availability of different sources of funds;
- effect of different sources of finance on company risk;
- direct and indirect costs of different sources of finance;
- effect of tax on the relative costs of equity and debt.

▌ Factors influencing the choice and mix of finance

- Gearing
- Taxation
- Political risk
- Currency risk

Gearing: its measurement and significance

Gearing (the amount of debt finance relative to the amount of equity finance) can be measured by the debt/equity ratio or by the capital gearing ratio, and market values, rather than book values, should be used when calculating gearing ratios. Industries with lower levels of business risk typically have higher levels of gearing than industries with higher levels of business risk. What is the significance of high levels of gearing?

▌ Increased volatility of equity returns

Increases in the interest paid by a company will make its profits and distributable earnings more volatile. This risk (financial risk) is borne by shareholders and the more debt a company has, the higher will be its financial risk.

▌ Increased possibility of bankruptcy

Bankruptcy risk, which is faced by all shareholders and debt holders, is the risk of a company failing to meet its interest payment commitments and subsequently going into liquidation.

▌ Reduced credibility on the stock exchange

Investors who see a company as highly geared will be reluctant to buy its shares or to offer it further debt, leading to a loss of financial credibility and a falling share price.

▌ Encouragement of short-termism

If a company has a high level of gearing, managers may focus on the short-term need to meet interest payments rather than the longer-term objective of wealth maximisation.

▌ The concept of an optimal capital structure

The lower a company's WACC, the higher the NPV of its future cash flows and therefore the higher its market value. Is there an optimal capital structure that minimises the WACC and therefore maximises the market value?

■ Gearing and the required rate of return

The cost of equity is always higher than the cost of debt as share-holders face higher levels of risk. Shareholders require a minimum return equal to the risk-free rate of return as well as a premium for business risk. The combination of the risk-free rate and the business risk premium represents the cost of equity of a company financed entirely by equity. If a company has debt finance, the cost of equity is increased by a premium for financial risk and this premium increases as gearing increases (Figure 9.3). At very high levels of gearing, a premium is also required for bankruptcy risk.

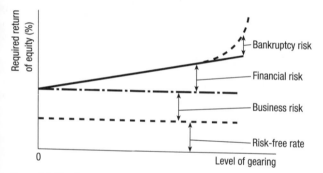

Figure 9.3 The determinants of a company's cost of equity finance

The cost of debt is fixed as gearing increases, since debt holders do not face financial risk. At very high levels of gearing, debt holders require a premium for bankruptcy risk.

The traditional approach to capital structure

Some simplifying assumptions are made:

■ no taxes exist;
■ perpetual debt finance and equity finance are available to companies;
■ capital structure can be changed without issue costs or redemption costs;
■ gearing up means replacing equity finance by debt finance;
■ companies pay out all distributable earnings as dividends;
■ business risk of a company is constant over time;
■ companies' earnings and hence dividends are constant over time.

In the traditional approach to capital structure, shareholders are indifferent to the addition of small amounts of debt, and so the WACC falls as gearing up begins. At high levels of gearing, both the cost of equity and the cost of debt increase due to bankruptcy risk. Between the extremes of using only equity finance and very high gearing, a minimum WACC (B) and an optimal capital structure (X) can therefore be found (see Figure 9.4).

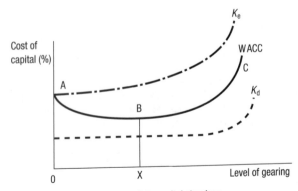

Figure 9.4 The traditional approach to capital structure

Miller and Modigliani (I): the net income approach

Miller and Modigliani (1958) said that:

- no optimal capital structure exists;
- WACC and market value are constant at all levels of gearing;
- market value depends on the expected performance and business risk of a company.

In addition to the assumptions made by the traditional approach, Miller and Modigliani assumed that capital markets are perfect (see Figure 9.5), so that bankruptcy risk could be ignored.

- There is a linear relationship between the cost of equity and financial risk (gearing).
- The cost of debt is constant and independent of the level of gearing.
- As a company gears up by replacing equity with debt, the benefit of using cheaper debt is exactly offset by the increasing cost of equity finance.

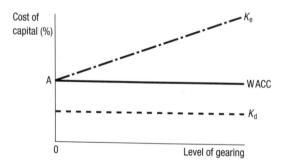

Figure 9.5 Miller and Modigliani's net operating income approach to capital structure

■ The arbitrage approach to capital structure

Miller and Modigliani used arbitrage theory to show that two companies, identical in every way except for their gearing levels, should have *identical average costs of capital*. The assumptions they made were challenged as being unrealistic.

- They assumed that individuals can borrow at the same rate as companies.
- They assumed that buying and selling securities involved no transaction costs.
- They assumed that taxation can be ignored.

Miller and Modigliani (II): corporate tax

Miller and Modigliani (1963) amended their earlier model by including the effect of corporate tax (Figure 9.6). The tax deductibility of interest payments implies that replacing equity with debt will shield more and more profit from corporate tax, and that WACC will decrease as gearing increases, since the after-tax cost of debt is lower than the before-tax cost of debt. The optimal capital structure is therefore 100% debt finance.

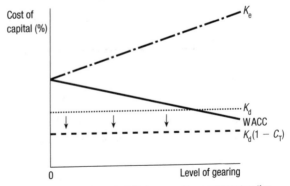

Figure 9.6 Miller and Modigliani (II), incorporating corporate taxation

Market imperfections

In practice, companies do not adopt an all-debt capital structure due to factors that undermine the tax advantages of debt finance – which Miller and Modigliani failed to take into account.

Bankruptcy costs

In a *perfect* capital market, bankruptcy risk does not exist. In reality, however, bankruptcy risk does exist and shareholders require increased compensation for facing it. Combining the tax shield advantage of increasing gearing with the bankruptcy costs associated with very high levels of gearing, an optimal capital structure emerges.

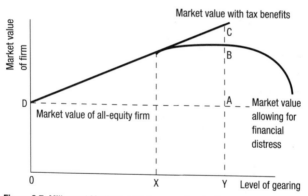

Figure 9.7 Miller and Modigliani (II), incorporating bankruptcy risk

In Figure 9.7:
AC = value of the tax shield
BC = cost of bankruptcy risk
AB = net benefit of the geared company.

While bankruptcy costs at high gearing levels clearly exist, the size of these costs and the level of gearing at which they become relevant are less clear.

▌Agency costs

Agency costs arise at high levels of gearing because shareholders, whose potential losses are limited, prefer a company to invest in high-risk/high-return projects, while debt holders seek to prevent investment in such projects, for example, through restrictive covenants or increased monitoring. These agency costs will reduce the tax shield benefits of higher gearing levels.

▌Tax exhaustion

At higher levels of gearing, many companies will have insufficient profits from which to gain the tax benefits represented by the tax shield.

Miller and personal taxation

Miller (1977) considered the relationship between personal tax and capital structure, and concluded that the WACC is independent of the level of gearing (as in Miller and Modigliani's first model), although he did not consider the effect of bankruptcy risk.

Pecking order theory

Pecking order theory suggests that there is a well-defined order of preference with respect to sources of finance when a company is financing long-term investment. In decreasing order of preference, these are:

- internal finance or retained earnings;
- bank borrowings;
- corporate bonds;
- new equity capital.

These preferences can be explained by several factors:

- issue costs;
- the ease with which sources of finance are accessed;
- ownership implications;
- asymmetry of information between the company and capital markets.

(A detailed discussion of optimal capital structure theory is given on pp. 281–93 in the textbook.)

Does an optimal capital structure exist? A conclusion

In practice, it is more likely that a range of capital structures exist with which a company can minimise its WACC (i.e. between P and Q in Figure 9.8), rather than one particular optimal capital structure that some academic theories might suggest. This implies that the WACC curve will be flatter in practice than the U-shaped curve of academic theories. It appears, therefore, that using sensible levels of debt in its capital structure can allow a company to enjoy the tax advantages of debt finance and a lower WACC, as its gearing does not lead to concern among its investors about possible bankruptcy.

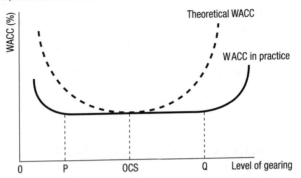

Figure 9.8 The relationship between the academic approach to optimal capital structure and the weighted average cost of capital in practice

Examination pointers

- ✔ The dividend growth model, the CAPM and the WACC are usually given in a formulae sheet in an exam, but you have to remember the meanings of all the symbols.

- ✔ You must be practised in calculating the costs of individual sources of finance and the WACC, since this topic is often examined and is a core area in corporate finance.

- ✔ Note that market values are always preferred to book values in calculating WACC.

- ✔ Learn the reasons why WACC can be used as a discount rate in investment appraisal in very limited circumstances (same business risk, same financial risk), and be prepared to calculate a CAPM-derived project-specific discount rate.

- ✔ The advantages and disadvantages of using the CAPM in investment appraisal is a popular exam discussion topic; therefore, it is well worth revising this area thoroughly.

✔ A discussion of the cost of capital for FDI, or the significance of the financing decision in FDI, is often linked with an FDI evaluation using NPV in a single exam question.

✔ The key corporate finance topic of optimal capital structure theory is a rich discussion area that can be illustrated by several diagrams, so being able to draw these diagrams accurately and explain them in detail can be a key to getting good marks if this topic is examined.

10
Dividend policy

Introduction

Dividend policy determines the return paid by a company to shareholders:

- dividend decisions, financing decisions and investment decisions are closely related;
- a decision made in one area will affect decisions in other areas;
- dividend decisions may take account of shareholders' views and expectations, as well as the relative cost and availability of finance to the company.

Dividends: operational and practical issues

Although a dividend is a 'distribution of after-tax profit', it is a cash payment made by a company to its shareholders. In the UK, the *total dividend* is the sum of the interim and final dividends. The final dividend needs shareholder approval and is paid after the end of the financial year.

- When a dividend is announced, the share price goes cum dividend (cum div) for a short period: anyone buying the share in this period gains the right to receive the dividend.

- When the shareholder list is closed, the share price goes ex-dividend (ex-div): if the share is bought after this date, the buyer will not receive the dividend, entitlement to which remains with the previous owner.
- On the ex-div date, the share price falls by the amount of the dividend paid, to reflect the change in intrinsic value.

■ Legal constraints

- Dividends can only be paid out of accumulated net realised profits.
- On occasion, the UK government has imposed direct restrictions on dividend payments.
- Dividend payments may be restricted by loan agreements or debt covenants.

■ Liquidity

Since dividends are cash payments, the dividend decision must reflect the company's ability to pay dividends, not just its profits.

■ Interest payment obligations

Since dividends are a distribution of after-tax profit, the level of dividends is limited by interest payment obligations and gearing commitments.

■ Investment opportunities

The decision to reduce dividend payments in order to finance investment opportunities depends on a number of factors:

- the attitude of shareholders and stock markets to a dividend reduction;
- the availability and cost of external sources of finance;
- the amount of funds needed relative to available distributable profits.

The effect of dividends on shareholder wealth

Dividend policy objectives should be consistent with the objective of maximising shareholder wealth and so a dividend should be paid only if it leads to such a wealth increase. Porterfield (1965) suggested that paying a dividend will increase shareholder wealth only when:

$$d_1 + P_1 > P_0$$

where: d_1 = cash value of dividend per share paid to shareholders

P_1 = expected ex-div share price

P_0 = share price before dividend was announced.

- d_1 is influenced by shareholders' marginal income tax rates;
- P_0 reflects market expectations of a company's performance before a dividend is paid;
- P_1 is influenced by any new information about a company signalled by the dividend.

Dividend irrelevance

Miller and Modigliani (1961) argued that share values depend on the level of earnings and not on the amount of earnings paid out as dividends (dividend decisions). They also argued that, as share values do not depend on capital structure (financing decisions), company value depends *only* on investment decisions, which determine earnings. Share values are therefore *independent* of the level of dividend paid by a company. They made the following assumptions:

- selling shares for cash incurs no transactions costs;
- issuing shares incurs no transactions costs;
- there are no corporate or personal taxes;
- capital markets are perfect.

Miller and Modigliani noted that rational investors are indifferent to whether they receive capital gains or dividends, and that a company's market value is maximised by an optimal investment policy.

- An optimal investment policy means investing in all projects with a positive NPV.
- In a perfect capital market there is no capital rationing to limit such a policy.
- Any additional finance needed for such a policy can be raised by issuing new shares.
- Any surplus cash left over after investing all positive NPV projects can be returned to shareholders as a residual dividend.

Miller and Modigliani did not argue that dividends are a residual payment, but argued that:

- the value of a company following an optimal investment policy is not affected by its dividend policy;
- the investment decision is independent from the dividend decision;
- the choice of dividend policy is really a choice of financing strategy.

Miller and Modigliani did not argue that shareholders were not concerned about whether they received a dividend or not, but that shareholders were indifferent to the *timing* of dividend payments.

- In a perfect capital market, the increase in the company's share price reflects exactly the incremental future income resulting from incremental invested capital.
- Shareholders who wanted cash if no dividend had been paid could, it was argued, create 'home-made' dividends by selling some of their shares whose value had increased.

(The complex argument for dividend irrelevancy is detailed on pp. 306–8 in the textbook.)

Dividend relevance

An alternative view to that of Miller and Modigliani is that dividend policy *does* affect share prices. Lintner (1956) and Gordon (1959) argued that dividends are preferred to capital gains because a dividend paid now is certain, whereas a future capital gain is uncertain.

- If investors prefer dividends to capital gains, dividend policy will influence share prices.
- Companies paying lower dividends will have lower share prices than companies paying higher dividends.

There are other arguments in support of dividend relevance.

Dividends are signals to investors

In a semi-strong form efficient capital market, information asymmetry exists between managers and shareholders, so it has been argued that dividend decisions can be seen as conveying new information about a company and its prospects.

- A dividend increase is usually seen as good news, although it could mean a shortage of positive NPV investments and a low level of future growth.
- A dividend decrease is usually seen as bad news, although it could mean investment in positive NPV projects and a higher level of future growth.
- Miller (1986) argued that the *difference* between the actual dividend and the market's expectation of the dividend was more important than the *direction* of the dividend change.

The clientele effect

It has been argued that shareholders are *not* indifferent about receiving dividends or capital gains.

- Some shareholders need dividends as a source of regular income.
- Preferences for dividends or capital gains may arise due to their different tax treatment.

- Preferences for dividends or capital gains means that investors are attracted to companies whose dividend policies satisfy their needs.
- Each company therefore builds up a clientele of shareholders satisfied by its dividend policy.

The implication of this 'clientele effect' is that a significant change in a company's dividend policy could dissatisfy its shareholders, leading to a fall in its share price.

■ The dividend growth model

The dividend growth model calculates the current market price of a share as the sum of its discounted future dividend payments, and so lends support to the dividend relevance view.

$$P_0 = \frac{D_1}{(1+r)} + \frac{D_1(1+g)}{(1+r)^2} + \frac{D_1(1+g)^2}{(1+r)^3} + ... + \frac{D_1(1+g)^{n-1}}{(1+r)^n}$$

where: P_0 = current ex div market price of the share
D_1 = declared dividend at time t_1
g = expected future growth rate of dividends
n = number of years for which the share is held
r = shareholders' required rate of return (cost of equity)

This equation can be simplified by assuming that the n tends towards infinity, giving:

$$P_0 = \frac{D_0(1+g)}{(r+g)} = \frac{D_1}{(r+g)}$$

This equation is the *dividend growth model* (DGM). The current dividend D_0 is usually known. The cost of equity can be calculated using the CAPM. The expected future dividend growth rate is hard to estimate. One way of predicting it is by looking at historical dividend growth rates.

Example

Calculating a share price using the DGM

Cost of equity: 15%

Current dividend: $D_0 = 80p$ per share

Previous dividends: 68p, 73p, 74p and 77p per share (most recent dividend last)

Historical dividend growth rate: $g = (80/68)^{0.25} - 1$
$$= 0.041 \text{ or } 4.1\%$$

Inserting D_0, g and r into the DGM:

$$P_0 = \frac{80(1+0.041)}{(0.15-0.041)} = \frac{83.28}{(0.015-0.041)} = £7.64$$

Problems with using the dividend growth model to value shares include the following:

- In reality, dividends do not grow smoothly and care must be taken in assuming that the historical dividend growth rate is an approximation of the future dividend growth rate.
- The model implies that if D_0 is zero, the share is worthless: in reality, dividend payments will probably begin in the future and the DGM can be applied to calculate a future share price that can be discounted to give a current share price.
- It is argued that the DGM fails to take capital gains into account by assuming an infinite holding period: again this is not really a problem since, if a share is sold, the price paid will be the present value of its expected future dividends on the selling date; future dividends and their present value are not affected by a change in ownership.
- It has been noted that the DGM makes no allowance for personal or other taxes: however, it can modified to include such tax effects.

In the model's favour, it can be argued:

- There may be no reason to assume that the historical dividend growth rate will change.
- Small errors in distant dividends are unlikely to be significant due to discounting.

Dividend relevance or irrelevance?

The unrealistic nature of Miller and Modigliani's assumptions can be highlighted.

- Transaction costs are not zero and so capital gains (via 'home-made dividends') are not a perfect substitute for dividends in cash flow terms.
- Taxation does exist in the real world, further distorting the equivalence of dividends and capital gains.
- New share issues do incur issue costs.
- Information is not free.

These shortcomings do not totally invalidate Miller and Modigliani's argument, and empirical research by Black and Scholes (1974) and by Miller and Scholes (1978) supports dividend irrelevance. In reality, dividend policy is seen as an important factor in determining the market price of shares:

- The reactions of institutional shareholders to proposed dividend cuts indicate that they consider dividend payments to be very important.
- Institutional investors needing income have been accused of putting pressure on companies to pay dividends they cannot really afford.

Dividend policies

Fixed percentage payout ratio policy

This is relatively easy to operate and clearly signals corporate performance, but reinvestment funds are limited and it is usually unsuitable if shareholders want stable dividends.

Zero dividend policy

This policy is easy to operate and may be adopted by newly-formed companies. It will be acceptable to only a minority of shareholders who prefer capital gains to dividends.

Constant or steadily increasing dividend

- A constant or increasing money-terms dividend may give a declining or increasing real-terms dividend.
- A constant or increasing real-terms dividend will usually give an increasing money-terms dividend.
- Dividend increases lag increases in longer-term sustainable earnings, since shareholders expect increasing dividends even when earnings decline.

Dividend policies in practice

Dividend policies are influenced by the nature of a company's business and by the nature of the company itself, and change over time as company circumstances and the economy change.

- Lower dividend payout ratios tend to occur where companies are capital intensive, have high business risk or have high financial risk.
- Higher dividend payout ratios tend to occur with mature companies or those with low reinvestment requirements.

(An illustration of corporate dividend policy can be seen on p. 317 in the textbook.)

Alternatives to cash dividends

■ Scrip dividend

This is a pro rata offer of additional ordinary shares as a partial or total alternative to a cash dividend and is treated as income for tax purposes. An *enhanced* scrip dividend is one whose value exceeds that of the cash dividend alternative, and shareholders choose the alternative that best suits their individual needs. There is a cash flow advantage to the company, as well as a slight decrease in gearing.

■ Share repurchases

Share repurchases are often used to return cash to ordinary shareholders in the UK:

- they require the prior approval of existing and potential shareholders;
- they enhance the value of the remaining shares;
- the return on capital employed will increase, as will earnings per share;
- the increase in financial risk is negligible.

Shares can be repurchased by a tender offer (an offer to all shareholders at a price set by the company), a stock market repurchase (where the repurchase price is not fixed) or an agency buy-back (from individual shareholders).

■ Special dividend

This is a one-off cash payment to all shareholders that is significantly higher than the dividend payments usually made by a company. Special dividends are not common and depend on the individual circumstances of a company.

■ Non-pecuniary benefits

These are also known as shareholder perks and are discounts on a company's goods and services, or the offer of complimentary goods and services, to qualifying shareholders.

Empirical evidence on dividend policy

- There is evidence that companies treat dividend decisions as separate from investment decisions, and that companies increase dividends gradually as earnings increase, in order to reduce the need for dividend decreases should earnings fall.
- Brennan (1970) proposed that share prices would change in order to give the same after-tax rate of return regardless of dividend policy, implying that companies could increase their share price by adopting lower levels of earnings distribution.
- Black and Scholes (1974) did not find a positive relationship between dividend yields and before-tax returns.
- Elton and Gruber (1970) found that high dividend shares were associated with lower marginal rates of income tax, supporting the existence of tax clienteles.
- Pettit (1977) and Crossland et al. (1991) also supported the existence of a clientele effect.
- Miller and Scholes (1978) showed that tax planning could negate the different tax treatment of dividends and capital gains, hence lending support to Miller and Modigliani's dividend irrelevance theory.
- Pettit (1972), Aharony and Swary (1980) and Kwan (1981) all concluded that dividend changes do convey new information to shareholders.

Examination pointers

- ✔ Understand the close relationship between the investment, financing and dividend decisions, and how the views of Miller and Modigliani on capital structure and dividend policy are focused on this close relationship.
- ✔ Operational and practical issues about dividends can be examined as a part question.

✔ The dividend irrelevance analysis of Miller and Modigliani is a popular discussion topic in examinations, so make sure you understand the reasons for their conclusions.

✔ The dividend relevance view is close to what is observed in the real world, where certainty is preferred to uncertainty and where capital markets are semi-strong form efficient rather than perfect.

✔ An understanding of dividend policies can help in analysing dividend performance.

✔ Alternatives to dividends usually play a minor role in dividend policy questions.

11

Mergers and takeovers

Introduction

Mergers and takeovers are a complex, integrated area of corporate finance:

- they are a strategic opportunity for acquiring companies and a threat to target companies;
- valuing target companies and estimating acquisition benefits can be difficult;
- takeover bids can be time-consuming and expensive;
- acquiring company shareholders may obtain little or no increase in wealth.

The terminology of mergers and takeovers

The terms 'merger' and 'takeover' can mean the same thing, but a merger is technically a combination of equal-sized companies, while a takeover is the acquisition of one company's ordinary shares by another company. Most acquisitions are takeovers rather than mergers. There are three types of takeover:

- Horizontal takeover, where the combining companies operate in the same industry and at the same stage of production.

- Vertical takeover, where the combining companies operate in the same industry and at different stages of production.
- Conglomerate takeover, where the combining companies operate in different industries.

Justifications for acquisitions

Acquisitions should increase the wealth of acquiring company shareholders, while mergers should increase the wealth of shareholders of both companies. Justifications or motives for acquisitions can be classified under several headings.

Economic justifications for acquisitions

The economic justification for acquisitions is that shareholder wealth increases because the combined company is worth more than the separate companies. If PV is present value and X and Y are the combining companies:

$$PV_{X+Y} > (PV_X + PV_Y)$$

Economic gains occur for many reasons.

Synergy

Synergy occurs when the business operations of two companies complement each other, so that the value of the combined operations is greater than the value of the separate operations. For example, synergy can arise through economies of scale. Synergy is difficult to quantify before an acquisition and hard to realise after an acquisition.

Economies of scale

The average cost per unit can be decreased because the scale of operations increases after an acquisition, for example, in a horizontal takeover.

Elimination of inefficient management

Economic benefits can arise if an acquisition results in inefficient target company managers being replaced by better managers from the acquiring company.

Entry to new markets

Acquisition can offer a quicker or cheaper way to enter new markets than internal growth.

To provide critical mass

Acquisition can help to achieve critical mass in key areas such as research and development.

As a means of providing growth

Acquisitions can offer a way of achieving corporate growth targets.

Market power and share

Horizontal acquisitions can increase market share while vertical acquisitions can increase power relative to suppliers and customers.

▊ Financial justifications for acquisitions

Acquisitions can be justified by the financial benefits they bring to shareholders.

Financial synergy

Financial synergy occurs if a company's cost of capital decreases as a result of an acquisition. The cost of capital can decrease if cash flow volatility decreases, for example, due to a lack of correlation between acquiring and target company cash flows in a conglomerate acquisition. This reduction in unsystematic business risk has no value to a shareholder with a diversified investment portfolio. The cost of capital can also decrease through size effects, such as scale economies in new finance issue costs, or a higher credit rating leading to lower interest rates.

Target undervaluation

Suggesting that a target company is undervalued implies that capital markets are inefficient. While empirical evidence supports market efficiency, difficulties in valuing companies leaves scope for undervaluation.

Tax considerations

A tax-exhausted company may benefit from acquiring a profitable company in order to realise tax-allowable benefits.

Increasing earnings per share

If an acquiring company has a higher price/earnings ratio than a target company and uses a share-for share offer, its post-acquisition earnings per share (EPS) can be higher than its pre-acquisition EPS, potentially leading to a higher share price through a process called bootstrapping. Increasing EPS, however, will not increase cash flows or shareholder wealth.

■ Managerial justifications for acquisitions

Acquisitions can occur because managers want to increase their own utility in terms of pay, power or job security, but from an agency problem perspective, such acquisitions will not increase shareholder wealth.

(There are many rationales for acquisitions, as shown on pp. 333–7 in the textbook.)

■ The case against acquisition

Referral to the Competition Commission

A Competition Commission referral can be expensive, time-consuming and reputation-damaging, and may result in the bid not being allowed to proceed.

Contested bid

The bidding company may have to pay a relatively high premium if a bid is contested.

Are mergers and takeovers beneficial?

In general, only target company shareholders and bidding company managers benefit from acquisitions, whereas acquiring company shareholders do not benefit.

The cost of financing a takeover
The method of financing an acquisition can have implications in terms of dividends, ownership structure, gearing level and issue costs.

Other difficulties
These can include:

- cultural problems;
- exchange rate risk (e.g. with cross-border acquisitions);
- taxation and legal issues;
- uncertain quality of acquired assets.

Trends in takeover activity

Acquisitions can occur in waves for a number of reasons:

- industry-specific reasons, such as scale economies, synergy, and market consolidation;
- finance-specific reasons, such as the state of the stock exchange and corporate liquidity levels;
- deregulation of capital and other markets.

Target company valuation

It is possible to calculate several different values for a company using either income-based or asset-based valuation methods.

Stock market value

- Number of issued ordinary shares multiplied by their market price;
- minimum price at which a target company can be bought;
- purchase price could be stock market value plus an acquisition premium;
- stock market value represents only marginal trading;
- limited usefulness if shares are traded infrequently or not at all.

■ Asset-based valuation methods

Net asset value (book value)

The net asset value (book value):

- is equal to: Non-current assets + Net current assets – Long-term debt;
- uses historical costs, which do not reflect current asset valuations;
- ignores intangible assets such as goodwill, human capital and brands;
- offers only a lower limit for the target company's value.

Net asset value (net realisable value)

This method uses net realisable value (liquidation value) rather than book value.

- The market value of the target company should be higher than its net realisable value.
- The net realisable values are difficult to determine in practice.
- The net asset value is a useful valuation method, perhaps, if the bidder intends to sell off part of the target.

Net asset value (replacement cost)

This method uses replacement cost rather than book value:

- Replacement cost estimates of asset values are more relevant than historical cost estimates
- Replacement costs are difficult to determine or use in practice.

■ Income-based valuation methods

Income-based values are useful if the acquirer intends to continue the business of the target company as a going concern and consider the additional income gained.

Earning yield value

$$\text{Earnings yield value} = \frac{\text{Annual maintainable expected earnings}}{\text{Required earnings yield}}$$

- This is a forward-looking value that encourages forecasting of future performance.
- A disadvantage here is uncertainty about the accuracy of the earnings figure.

Price/earnings ratio valuation

This value is found by multiplying annual maintainable distributable earnings by an appropriate price/earnings (P/E) ratio.

- Possible P/E ratios include the bidder's P/E ratio, the target company's P/E ratio, a weighted average P/E ratio or a sector average P/E ratio.
- Values produced fluctuate widely according to the P/E ratio applied.
- Forecasting future earnings is difficult.

Dividend growth model

The present value of future dividends is given by the dividend growth model:

$$P_0 = \frac{D_0(1 + g)}{(r - g)}$$

where: D_0 = current total dividend payment
        g = expected annual growth rate of dividends
        r = required rate of return of the company's shareholders.

- A major drawback is the sensitivity of the model to the expected dividend growth rate.
- The model can be used to value a minority shareholding in a target company.

Discounted cash flow valuation

The maximum amount the acquirer should pay is the difference between the present values of its pre- and post-acquisition cash flows:

$$PV_{X+Y} - PV_Y$$

This should be equal to the present value of the incremental cash flows gained by the acquirer.

- Future cash flows and an appropriate discount rate must be calculated.
- The evaluation period and a terminal value must be determined.
- The discount rate should reflect the risk characteristics of the incremental cash flows, for example by using the CAPM.

(Many students struggle with valuation, so study carefully pp. 341–8 in the textbook.)

The financing of acquisitions

The financial implications of an acquisition depend on the financing method used, which must satisfy the needs of both sets of shareholders if a bid is to be successful. The popularity of financing methods has changed over time.

Cash offers

The bidding company uses cash to acquire the shares of the target company. Advantages of this financing method include:

- Target shareholders are certain of the amount they will receive, which is not the case with a share-for-share offer.
- The control of acquiring company shareholders is not diluted.

Disadvantages include:

- Target shareholders may be liable to capital gains tax on share disposals.
- The bidding company may find it difficult to raise large amounts of debt.
- Leveraged acquisitions can significantly increase acquiring company gearing, although post-acquisition disposals can reduce the debt burden.

∎ Share-for-share offers

The bidding company offers a fixed number of its shares in exchange for target company shares. Advantages of share-for-share offers include:

- Target company shareholders can retain an equity interest in their company.
- Target company shareholders do not incur a capital gains tax liability from share disposals.

Disadvantages include:

- Share-for-share offers are more expensive than cash offers to the acquiring company.
- Issuing new shares will dilute the control of existing shareholders.

∎ Vendor placings and vendor rights issues

- A vendor placing involves offering shares to target shareholders, while arranging at the same time for the shares to be placed with institutional investors in exchange for cash.
- A vendor rights issue involves offering shares to target shareholders, while arranging at the same time for the shares to be sold to acquiring company shareholders in a rights issue.

■ Security packages

It is rare for securities other than ordinary shares (e.g. bonds or preference shares) to be offered to target shareholders by the bidder.

■ Mixed bids

A mixed bid is a share-for-share offer with a cash alternative, and is a popular method of financing acquisitions. Mixed bids are seen as allowing target company shareholders to select the payment method that best suits their liquidity preferences and tax positions, as well as satisfying Rule 9 of the City Code on Takeovers and Mergers.

Strategic and tactical issues

The strategic process of acquiring a target company is as follows:

1 Confirm that acquisition is the desired strategic choice.
2 Identify suitable target companies.
3 Obtain information about target companies.
4 Value each target company and decide on the maximum prices for each alternative.
5 Select the most appropriate target company.
6 Decide on the best way to finance the acquisition.
7 Decide on the tactics to be used.

The significance of different levels of shareholding must be understood: for example, owning 50% of a target company's shares gives the power to control its decision-making process.

■ Merger regulation and control

Mergers and acquisitions are governed by legal controls (antitrust regulation) and by self-regulatory controls.

Legal controls

- UK acquisitions come under the Enterprise Act (2002).
- The Office of Fair Trading (OFT) carries out initial reviews of acquisitions and can refer those that may substantially reduce competition to the Competition Commission (CC).
- Investigations by the CC usually take up to six months.

The OFT, in deciding if an acquisition should be referred, considers the public interest in terms of:

- effective competition within an industry;
- the interests of consumers, purchasers and users of goods and services with respect to quality, price and choice;
- cost reduction and introducing new products and techniques.

Self-regulatory controls

Acquisitions in the UK fall under the non-statutory self-regulation of the Takeover Panel via the City Code on Takeovers and Mergers. This Code:

- is based on 10 general principles and 38 more specific rules;
- applies to all listed and unlisted public companies resident in the UK;
- ensures that target company shareholders are treated equitably in the bidding process;
- lays down a strict timetable to be followed by all takeover bids.

▌ The bidding process

The City Code includes the following procedures.

- The bidding company must notify its potential target 5 days after it has built up a 3% holding of its shares (in order to discourage dawn raids).
- Once 30% of the target company's shares are held, the bidding company has to make a cash offer to all remaining shareholders.
- The bidding company must inform the target company board of the nature and terms of its offer, and the target company board must pass details of the bid to its shareholders.

- Once offers have been posted they are open for 21 days, extendable by 14 days if any amendments to the offer are made.
- An offer becomes unconditional when the bidding company has obtained more than 50% of the target company's shares.

■ Bid defences

The target company board of directors should only reject a bid if it is not in the best interests of their shareholders. Bid defences may be employed before or after a bid is received.

Pre-bid defences

Efficient management of a company in order to maximise shareholder wealth is the best constructive pre-bid defence against a takeover bid. This form of defence is supported by:

- improving operational efficiency;
- examining asset portfolios and making necessary divestments;
- ensuring good investor relations.

Obstructive pre-bid defences are intended to make a company both difficult and expensive to acquire, and are usually not consistent with shareholder wealth maximisation. Examples are:

- restructuring of equity, including share repurchase schemes and poison pills;
- management retrenchment devices, such as golden parachutes;
- strategic defences, such as share cross-holdings with friendly companies.

Post-bid defences

- Rejection of the initial offer;
- a pre-emptive circulation to shareholders;
- formulation of a defence document;
- profit announcements and forecasts;
- dividend increase announcements;
- revaluation of assets or capitalisation of intangible assets;
- searching for a white knight;

- pac-man defence;
- acquisitions and divestments, such as the crown jewels defence.

Divestment

Reasons for divestment

Divestment can occur for a number of reasons, including:

- raising cash, which could be used to ease liquidity problems or reduce gearing;
- focusing on core strategic activities;
- generating synergy by divesting assets into the hands of specialist managers;
- selling of surplus assets after an acquisition (asset stripping);
- divesting attractive assets after receiving a takeover bid (crown jewels defence).

Divestment strategies

- Sell-offs occur when companies sell off part of their business to a third party.
- Spin-offs (demergers) involve a pro rata distribution of a subsidiary's shares to a parent company's shareholders, so although the structure of the parent company changes, ownership of the assets does not. The benefits of a spin-off can include:
  1 creating a clearer management structure and encouraging more efficient asset usage;
  2 facilitating future corporate restructuring with respect to the demerged company;
  3 enhancing the value of the company as a whole by reversing the conglomerate discount.
- Management buyouts (MBOs) involve existing managers buying part or all of a business from its parent company, while management buy-ins (MBIs) involve a sale to an external management team.

■ Management buyouts

The reasons for an MBO being preferred to other divestment methods include:

- securing the co-operation of the subsidiary's management;
- the MBO team believes it can turn around a loss-making situation;
- the MBO team feel divestment will correct marginalisation relative to the group as a whole.

MBO financing

The MBO team will have insufficient funds to finance the purchase and will require external finance, usually a mixture of debt and equity. If a very high proportion of debt finance is used, the term 'leveraged buyout' is used. MBO financing sources include:

- ordinary equity provided by the MBO team and venture capitalists: the MBO team prefer to retain control, while venture capitalists see equity as a medium-term investment with profit gained through, for example, a stock market flotation;
- debt finance provided by venture capitalists or banks via term loans or bonds;
- mezzanine finance, which is unsecured debt finance that is less risky than ordinary equity, but more risky than secured debt.

Major suppliers of finance will usually require representation at board level in order to protect their investment from a strategic perspective.

The difficulties faced by MBOs

To gain assurance that the MBO will be a success, suppliers of MBO finance will consider:

- managerial expertise and quality;
- reasons for the sale of the business;
- the future prospects of the MBO company;
- the stake taken by the MBO team.

Problems faced by the MBO on the road to success include:

- how to provide, internally, business services previously provided by the parent;
- determining a fair price for the MBO;
- complicated tax and legal considerations;
- maintaining relationships with previous customers and suppliers;
- finding reinvestment or refinancing funds;
- maintaining employee pension rights;
- changing work practices in order to turn around corporate performance.

(Mergers and takeovers are often big news, as seen in Vignette 11.7 on p. 364 in the textbook.)

Private equity

Private equity firms use pooled private equity investment funds and additional debt finance to buy controlling stakes in companies, including venture capital investments and MBOs. The managerial expertise of the private equity firm is then used to maximise cash flow generation with the aim of reselling an acquired company at a profit in three to five years' time.

Empirical research on acquisitions

The economy

- Acquisitions have at best a neutral effect and there are no extreme efficiency gains.
- While economic wealth may not increase, some parties may benefit at the expense of others.

■ The shareholders of the companies involved

■ Accounting surveys showed that acquisitions are unprofitable for acquiring companies.

■ Event studies using the CAPM show that target company shareholders have significant positive returns, while acquiring company shareholders usually have insignificant gains or losses. Target company shareholder gains arise from the bid premium received.

■ Many surveys concluded that acquisitions are not wealth creating, but transfer wealth from acquiring company shareholders to the target company shareholders.

■ Managers and employees of acquiring and target companies

Acquiring company managers experience increased utility from successful takeovers, while target company managers and target employees tend to lose out.

■ Financial institutions

Financial institutions involved in advisory roles in the acquisition process gain financially by selling services to both bidding and target companies.

■ Other findings

Some studies have reported other findings:

■ Diversification destroys value, whereas increasing focus on core activities conserves value.

■ Acquisitions aimed at building monopoly power did not enhance acquirer performance.

■ Acquirers whose CEOs hold a larger proportion of equity shares make acquisitions that perform better compared with acquisitions where CEOs have a lower stake.

■ 'Glamour-buying' acquiring companies were more likely to destroy wealth compared to acquirers who acquired underperforming target companies.

Examination pointers

✔ Justifications for mergers and acquisitions are often examined as a discussion topic and can be linked to merger waves.

✔ Understanding of valuation methods is aided by regular practice of past exam questions and valuation is a key stage in the acquisition process.

✔ Financing methods can be examined from both a numerical and a discussion point of view.

✔ While the regulatory framework of mergers and acquisitions can be complex, antitrust regulation reflects the basic principles of public interest and fairness to shareholders.

✔ Management buyouts can be examined as a topic in their own right, with questions looking at financing, company valuation and shareholder wealth.

✔ An understanding of empirical research on mergers and acquisitions can help in most discussion questions in this area.

12
Risk management

Introduction

Exchange rate risk management is important to companies with international operations because many exchange rates are volatile. Interest rate risk management is important to companies with debt finance because of the cost to companies of interest rate changes. Companies need to understand the financial risks they face and how to manage or hedge these risks.

Interest rate risk

- A company with mainly floating rate debt faces the risk that interest rates may rise, increasing financial risk and affecting cash flows adversely.
- A company with mainly fixed rate debt faces the risk that interest rates may fall, decreasing its competitive advantage compared with companies with mainly variable rate borrowing.
- A company with floating rate investments faces the risk of interest rates falling, while a company with fixed rate investments faces the risk of interest rates rising.

▌ Basis risk

- Basis risk arises if a company's floating rate assets and liabilities have floating rates that are not determined using the same basis.

▌ Gap exposure

- Gap risk arises if a company's floating rate assets and liabilities have floating rates that are revised over different time periods.

Exchange rate risk

▊ Spot and forward rates

- The spot rate is the exchange rate for buying or selling a currency immediately.
- The forward rate fixes the exchange rate for buying or selling a currency in the future.

▌ Transaction risk

This is the risk that the domestic currency value of *short-term* foreign currency transactions may change due to exchange rate movements.

- Companies expecting foreign currency receipts are concerned about the risk of the foreign currency depreciating against the domestic currency.
- Companies needing to pay future foreign currency liabilities are concerned about the risk of the foreign currency appreciating against the domestic currency.

▌ Translation risk

This is the risk that, in the consolidation of accounts, a company may experience a loss or a gain due to exchange rate movements when translating foreign currency-denominated assets, liabilities and profits into the domestic currency.

- Translation losses or gains are only on paper and do not represent actual cash flows.
- Translation risk may affect the views of investors and financial institutions about a company.

■ Economic risk

This is the risk of long-term exchange rate movements undermining a company's international competitiveness or reducing the NPV of its business operations. It is a more general exchange rate risk than transaction and translation risk, and is almost impossible to avoid.

Internal risk management

Interest rate and exchange rate risk can be hedged internally by the way in which a company structures its assets and liabilities. Internal hedging is cheaper than external hedging, but of limited effect.

■ Internal management of interest rate risk

Interest rate risk can be hedged internally by smoothing or matching.

Smoothing
Smoothing involves maintaining a balance between fixed rate and floating rate debt.

- If interest rates rise, the increasing cost of floating rate debt is cancelled by the lower relative cost of fixed rate debt.
- If interest rates fall, the higher relative cost of fixed rate debt is cancelled out by the decreasing cost of floating rate debt.

Matching
This hedging method involves matching liabilities and assets with a common interest rate. As interest rates change, the increasing cost of one is offset by the decreasing cost of the other. Matching is mainly used by financial institutions.

▮ Internal management of exchange rate risk

Internal hedging normally applies to transaction risk and translation risk.

Matching

- ▪ To hedge translation risk, foreign currency assets and liabilities could be matched.
- ▪ Matching income and expenditure in the same currency can hedge transaction risk.

▮ Netting

Companies can net off foreign currency transactions that occur at the same time and in the same currency, and hedge only the net exposure.

▮ Leading and lagging

Foreign currency payments can be made at the beginning (leading) or after the end (lagging) of the credit period, depending on a company's expectation of future exchange rate movements.

▮ Invoicing in the domestic currency

An exporter could invoice in its own currency and thereby transfer the exchange rate risk to the importer, although this hedging method may not be commercially possible.

▮ External risk management

There are many methods of hedging exchange rate risk externally.

▮ Hedging using forward contracts

There are two types of forward contract.

- ▪ A forward rate agreements (FRA) is a binding contract that fixes in advance either a future borrowing rate or a future deposit rate on a nominal principal for a fixed period.

- A forward exchange contract (FEC) is a binding contract that fixes in advance an exchange rate on a specified quantity of foreign currency for delivery or purchase on an agreed date.

Advantages of forward contracts include:

- they can be tailor-made as to maturity and size in order to meet company requirements;
- unlike financial futures, they do not require the payment of initial or variation margin;
- unlike options, they do not require payment of an initial premium;
- they protect against the risk of adverse exchange rate or interest rate movements.

Disadvantages of forward contracts include:

- they are not standardised, and so cannot be closed out like futures and options;
- unlike options, they do not allow a company to take advantage of favourable movements in exchange rates or interest rates.

Example

Forward rate agreement

Borrowing: £5.6m in 3 months' time for a period of 6 months
Current interest rate: 6%
FRA: 6.5% on £5.6m for 6 months starting in 3 months' time
    (3 v 9 FRA)

Interest rate after 3 months is 7.5%:
Company pays 7.5% on its £5.6m loan and recieves a compensating payment from the bank of £28 000 (1% × £5.6m × 6/12), so its effective interest rate is 6.5%.

Interest rate after 3 months is 5%:
Company pays 5% on its £5.6m loan and makes a compensating payment to the bank of £42 000 (1.5% × £5.6m × 6/12), so its effective interest rate is 6.5%.

▌ Hedging using the money markets and eurocurrency markets

Money market hedges are also called cash market hedges.

- Interest rate risk can be hedged by borrowing in advance and placing borrowed funds on deposit until needed.
- Exchange rate risk can be hedged by using the eurocurrency markets to set up the opposite foreign currency transaction to the one being hedged.

Example

Money market hedge

Future receipt: $180 000 in 3 months' time
Current spot rate: $1.65/£
Annual dollar borrowing rate: 7%
Annual sterling deposit rate: 6%

Need to create future dollar liability, so borrow dollars now:
Three-month dollar borrowing rate = $7 \times 3/12 = 1.75\%$
Dollars borrowed now = $180\,000/1.0175 = \$176\,904$
Sterling value of these dollars at current spot rate =
    £107 215 = $176\,904/1.65$
Three-month sterling deposit rate = $6 \times 3/12 = 1.5\%$
Value of sterling deposit in 3 months' time = £108 823 =
    £107 215 × 1.015

The hedge receipt of £108 823 can be compared with the sterling receipt expected from an FEC to find the cheapest hedging method.

Futures contracts

A futures contract is an agreement to buy or sell a standard quantity of a specified financial instrument or foreign currency at a future date at a price agreed between two parties.

- Like traded options, financial futures are standardised contracts.
- Unlike traded options, futures are a binding contract as regards execution.
- Futures require both initial margin and variation margin.
- The need for variation margin arises as exchange rates or interest rates change, because futures are 'marked to market' on a daily basis.

Using futures contracts to hedge interest rate risk

- Companies *buy* futures to hedge against a fall in interest rates and *sell* futures to hedge against a rise in interest rates.
- Interest rate futures run in 3-month cycles (March, June, September and December).
- Futures are priced by subtracting the interest rate from 100 (e.g. a futures price of 93 reflects an interest rate of 7%).
- Profits or losses on a futures contract are calculated from changes in the futures price.
- Price changes are given in ticks (one basis point or 0.01% of the contract price): a one-tick change on a 3-month £500 000 interest rate future is £12.50 (i.e. £500 000 × 0.0001 × 3/12).

(Evaluating futures hedges can be tricky: see pp. 391–4 in the textbook for more details.)

Example

Using interest rate futures

Borrowing: £500 000 in 3 months' time for 3 months
Current interest rate: 10% and interest rates are expected to rise
Interest rate hedge: sell one £500 000 interest rate future at 90

Interest rate after 3 months is 13% and futures price is 87

Close out position by buying one contract at 87
Gain on futures = 300 ticks or £3750 (300 × £12.50)
Increase in borrowing cost = £3750 (500 000 × 0.03 × 1/4)

Interest rate hedge has exactly offset the higher borrowing cost (perfect hedge).

In reality, changes in futures prices do not exactly reflect interest rate changes (basis risk) and so hedges are unlikely to be 'perfect'.

■ Using futures contracts to hedge exchange rate risk

Example

Using US currency futures

Expected receipt: $300 000 by UK company in 3 months' time
Spot rate: 1.54–1.55 $/£ and sterling is expected to appreciate against the dollar
Currency futures: US-traded sterling futures for £62 500 priced at $1.535
Hedge: *buy* US sterling futures to allow delivery of foreign currency (sterling)
Sterling value of dollar receipt = $300 000/1.535 = £195 440
Futures needed = £195 440/62 500 = 3.13 contracts
Buying 3 contracts will deliver £187 500 (62 500 × 3) in exchange for $287 813 (187 500 × 1.535)

Surplus of $12187 can be sold at spot or via a forward contract

Futures allow UK company to lock into $1.535/£ exchange rate

Company has underhedged due to standardised nature of futures contracts.

■ Advantages and disadvantages of using futures to hedge risk

Advantages of hedging with futures:

- Unlike options, futures do not require payment of an initial premium.
- Unlike forward contracts, futures are tradable and have transparent prices.
- Contracts are marked to market on a daily basis.

Disadvantages of hedging using futures:

- Cash is needed for initial margin and variation margin.
- Advantage cannot be taken of favourable changes in interest rates and exchange rates.
- It is difficult to construct a perfect hedge.
- Basis risk will reduce hedge efficiency.

Options

Currency and interest rate options give the right, but not the obligation, to borrow or lend at a specific interest rate, or to buy or sell foreign currency at a specific exchange rate.

- Option holders can benefit from favourable interest rate and exchange rate changes.
- A non-refundable premium must be paid when the option is acquired.

■ Over-the-counter options

OTC options are bought from financial institutions and are tailor-made to company needs in terms of principal, time period, currency rate or interest rate.

- An interest rate cap guarantees a maximum interest rate to be paid by a company.
- An exchange rate cap guarantees a minimum domestic currency receipt from a future foreign currency receipt.
- An interest rate floor guarantees a minimum interest rate to be received by a company.
- An exchange rate floor guarantees a maximum domestic currency cost for a future foreign currency payment.
- A collar is the combination of a cap and a floor and keeps an interest rate or exchange rate between an upper and lower limit.
- A collar can be cheaper than using caps or floors on their own.

■ Traded options

Traded options are standardised in terms of principal amount and the maturity date.

- Traded options run in 3-month cycles (March, June, September and December).
- Put options give the right to sell currency or to lend at a fixed rate.
- Call options carry the right to buy currency or to borrow at a fixed rate.
- American options are exercisable up to and on their expiry date.
- European options are exercisable only on their expiry date.

(Evaluating option hedges needs careful study: see pp. 394–9 in the textbook for more details.)

■ Using traded options to hedge interest rate risk

Interest rate option contracts use futures contracts as the underlying asset and futures positions can be closed out by buying or selling contracts.

Example

Using interest rate options

Borrowing: £2m in 3 months' time for 3 months
Current (15 December) 3-month LIBOR rate: 6% and interest
  rates are expected to rise
15 March LIBOR sterling put option contracts: £0.5m each,
  strike price 94, 0.17 per contract
Hedge: buy 4 March sterling put option contracts
Cost of 4 sterling put options = 17 ticks $\times$ 4 $\times$ £12.50 = £850

Interest rate after 3 months is 8% and futures price is 92

Company exercises put option contracts to sell 4 futures at 94
Company closes out position by buying 4 futures at 92
Gain on futures = 200 ticks $\times$ 4 $\times$ £12.50 = £10 000
Increase in cost of borrowing = 2% $\times$ £2m $\times$ 1/4 = £10 000

Put option contracts have guaranteed a maximum borrowing
rate of 6%.

■ Using traded options to hedge exchange rate risk

Example

Using exchange rate options

Expected receipt: $1m by UK company in 3 months' time
Spot rate (19 December): $1.65/£, sterling expected to
  appreciate against the dollar

US-traded sterling currency options for £62 500, exercise price
$1.65, cost 7c/£

Hedge: *buy* US sterling call options, giving the right but not
the obligation to buy foreign currency (sterling)

Sterling value of expected receipt = $1m/1.65 = £606 061

Call option contracts needed = £606 061/62 500 = 9.7 or 10
contracts (overhedge)

Cost of 10 call option contracts = 62 500 × 10 × 0.07 = $43 750

Worst case: exchange dollar income at $1.72/£ (i.e. $1.65/
£ plus 7c/£ premium)

If spot rate in 3 months is below $1.65/£, will exchange dollar
income at spot

■ Factors affecting the price of traded options

Calculating option premiums is complex, as options prices are
affected by many factors.

Strike price
As the strike price increases, call option prices rise and put
option prices fall.

Changes in interest and exchange rates
As interest rates increase, interest rate call option prices rise and
put option prices fall.

Volatility of interest rates and exchange rates
Both call and put option prices rise as interest rate and exchange
rate volatility increases.

Time to expiry of the option
The longer the time to expiry, the more valuable an option will be
due to time value.

■ Advantages and disadvantages of hedging with options

Advantages of hedging with options:

- Options allow holders to benefit from favourable exchange and interest rate changes.
- Options are useful where a transaction is expected, but not certain.

Disadvantages of hedging with options:

- Unlike forward contracts and futures, options require payment of an up-front premium.
- Due to their standardised nature, it is difficult to create a perfect hedge using options.

Swaps

Swaps allow companies to benefit from their comparative advantages in different debt markets and to hedge interest rate and exchange rate exposures.

- Banks can warehouse swaps until a counterparty can be found.
- Swaps can be used to lock into interest rates and exchange rates for much longer periods than traded options, forward contracts or financial futures.

■ Interest rate swaps

An interest rate swap is an exchange of interest obligations or receipts in the same currency, on an agreed notional principal, for an agreed period of time.

Example

Plain vanilla interest rate swap

Company A can borrow fixed rate debt at 10% and floating rate at LIBOR

Company B can borrow fixed rate debt at 11% and floating rate debt at LIBOR + 0.2%

Company A has a comparative advantage in fixed rate debt, Company B in floating rate debt

Company A wants to borrow floating rate and Company B wants to borrow fixed rate debt

The difference between fixed rates is 1% and the difference between floating rates is 0.2%

Net benefit to be shared = 1% − 0.2% = 0.8% or 0.4% each (if shared equally)

Company A will pay a floating rate of LIBOR − 0.4% after the swap

Company B will pay a fixed rate of 10.6% after the swap

- Interest rate swaps can be used to hedge interest rate risk or to achieve a target mix of fixed and floating rate debt.
- In practice, the bank's arrangement fee will decrease the net benefit.
- Rather than swapping interest payments, balancing payments are made.

▌Currency swaps

A currency swap is an exchange of principal and interest payments in different currencies over an agreed time period. It allows a company to gain the use of funds in a foreign currency, while avoiding exchange rate risk on the principal or servicing payments.

- When the swap matures, the principal amounts are re-exchanged at the par exchange rate used at the start of the swap.

- In addition to the information in an interest rate swap, a currency swap will specify the currency to be paid, the currency to be received and the exchange rate to be used.
- An interest rate swap is implicit in every currency swap.

■ Advantages and disadvantages of hedging with swaps

Advantages of hedging with swaps:

- Swaps allow interest and exchange rate risk to be hedged for long periods of time.
- Swap arrangement fees are less than the premiums paid on options.
- Swaps are more flexible than traded derivatives as to principal and duration.

Disadvantages of hedging with swaps:

- Swaps do not give benefit from favourable exchange and interest rate movements.
- If a swap counterparty defaults, liability remains with the original borrower.

▌Issues in interest and exchange risk management

■ The need for a risk management strategy

- Hedging strategy formulation rests on formulating objectives, identifying and measuring risks, and selecting hedging methods.
- The consequences of inappropriate hedging can be very serious for a company.

(Vignette 12.4 on page 405 in the textbook illustrates the dangers of inappropriate hedges.)

The objectives of hedging policy

Companies must clearly define the objectives of their hedging policy. If the treasury department is a cost centre, hedging is a way of reducing risk and providing a service. If the treasury is a profit centre, speculating with derivatives may be encouraged.

Identifying and quantifying the risk exposure

- Interest and exchange rate risk exposures must be identified and quantified before hedging strategies can be implemented.
- A choice could be made between selective hedging or continuous hedging, depending on expectations about changes in exchange rates and interest rates.

Time horizon of hedging policy

Risk may be hedged on a short- or long-term basis.

Selection of hedging method

Internal hedging methods are used to hedge as much interest and exchange rate risk as possible. External hedging methods can be used for any remaining exposure. Factors to consider in selecting hedging methods include:

- Tailor-made derivatives can be used for non-standard exposures.
- Options can be used where the direction of interest or exchange rate movements is not completely certain.
- Bank-created products may be more appropriate where experience and knowledge about traded derivatives is lacking.

∎ The pros of risk management

Exchange rate and interest rate risk should be hedged when the expected benefits outweigh the hedging costs. There are a number of expected benefits of hedging:

- maintaining competitiveness;
- reduction of bankruptcy risk;
- restructuring of capital obligations;
- reduction in the volatility of corporate cash flows;
- enhancement of companies' debt capacity.

■ The cons of risk management

There are a number of potential problems that may arise with hedging, as follows:

- the complicated nature of hedging instruments;
- the costs associated with derivatives;
- the risks associated with using external hedging instruments;
- the complicated financial reporting and tax treatments of derivatives.

Diversification by shareholders may be superior to hedging

If shareholders diversify away interest and exchange rate risk by holding a diversified portfolio of shares, corporate hedging costs can be saved.

■ Managing the use of derivatives

If used properly, derivatives can bring real benefits to companies. Risk management policies must refer specifically to:

- the types of derivatives that can be used;
- limits on the volume and value of derivative transactions allowed;
- the need for a regular review of a company's derivative positions;
- systems and procedures to prevent unauthorised dealing.

Political risk

Political risk is the possibility of a multinational company being affected significantly by foreign country political events. It can be favourable or unfavourable.

■ Assessment of political risk

Macro-assessment of political risk is on a country-wide basis and can lead to political risk indices, by which countries can be ranked. Macro-assessment should be complemented by micro-assessment of political risk, which is from the perspective of the investor's business. Political risk can be assessed in several ways:

- checklist approach;
- delphi technique;
- quantitative analysis;
- inspection visits.

Policies to manage political risk

Political risk can be managed in several ways:

- insurance against political risk;
- negotiation of agreements;
- financing and operating policies.

Examination pointers

✔ Make sure you understand and use the terminology and concepts of risk management when answering exam questions, since the examiner is looking for this.

✔ Exam questions often ask you to discuss the relative merits of different hedging methods: hedge internally before hedging externally and learn about the range of hedging methods.

✔ Calculations to find the cheapest hedging method are common, especially with questions about hedging exchange rate risk.

✔ Using derivatives to manage interest and exchange rate risk is an activity that must be managed in order to avoid potentially serious problems for a company.

✔ Risk management is a requirement for all companies; therefore, they must have in place systems that identify, quantify, hedge and monitor the risk to which they are exposed.

References

Aharony, J. and Swary, I. (1980) 'Quarterly dividend and earnings announcements and stock holders' returns: an empirical analysis', *Journal of Finance*, Vol. 35, March, pp. 1–12.

Alexander, S. (1961) 'Price movements in speculative markets: trends or random walks', *Industrial Management Review*, May, pp. 7–26.

Beechey, M., Gruen, D. and Vickery, J. (2000) 'The efficient market hypothesis: a survey', Research Discussion Paper, Economic Research Department, Reserve Bank of Australia.

Black, E. and Scholes, M. (1974) 'The effects of dividend yield and dividend policy on common stock prices and returns', *Journal of Financial Economics*, Vol. 1, pp. 1–22.

Brennan, M. (1970) 'Taxes, market valuation and corporate financial policy', *National Tax Journal*, Vol. 23, pp. 417–27.

Crossland, M., Dempsey, M. and Mozier, P. (1991) 'The effect of cum and ex dividend changes on UK share prices', *Accounting and Business Research*, Vol. 22, No. 85, pp. 47–50.

Elton, E. and Gruber, M. (1970) 'Marginal stockholder tax rates and the clientele effect', *Review of Economics and Statistics*, Vol. 52, pp. 68–74.

Fama, E. (1965) 'The behaviour of stock market prices', *Journal of Business*, January, pp. 34–106.

Fama, E. (1970) 'Efficient capital markets: a review of theory and empirical work', *Journal of Finance*, Vol. 25, 383–417.

Gordon, M. (1959) 'Dividends, earnings and stock prices', *Review of Economics and Statistics*, Vol. 41, 99–105.

Hawawini, G. and Vora, A. (1982) 'Yield approximations: an historical perspective', *Journal of Finance*, Vol. 37, March, pp. 145–56.

Kendall, R. (1953) 'The analysis of economic time series, part 1: prices', *Journal of the Royal Statistical Society*, Vol. 69, pp. 11–25.

Kwan, C. (1981) 'Efficient market tests of the information content of dividend announcements: critique and extension', *Journal of Financial and Quantitative Analysis*, Vol. 16, June, pp. 193–206.

Lintner, J. (1956) 'Distribution of incomes of corporations among dividends, retained earnings and taxes', *American Economic Review*, Vol. 46, pp. 97–113.

Magnus, F.J. (2008) 'Capital market efficiency: an analysis of weak form efficiency on the Ghana stock exchange', *Journal of Money*, Investment and Banking, Issue 5, pp. 5–12.

Megginson, W.L. (1997) *Corporate Finance Theory*, Reading, MA: Addison–Wesley.

Miller, M. (1977) 'Debt and taxes', *Journal of Finance*, Vol. 32, pp. 261–75.

Miller, M. (1986) 'Behavioural rationality in finance: the case of dividends', *Journal of Business*, Vol. 59, pp. 451–68.

Miller, M. and Modigliani, F. (1958) 'The cost of capital, corporation finance and the theory of investment', *American Economic Review*, Vol. 48, pp. 261–96.

Miller, M. and Modigliani, F. (1961) 'Dividend policy, growth and the valuation of shares', *Journal of Business*, Vol. 34, pp. 411–33.

Miller, M. and Modigliani, F. (1963) 'Taxes and the cost of capital: a correction', *American Economic Review*, Vol. 53, pp. 433–43.

Miller, M. and Scholes, M. (1978) 'Dividends and taxes', *Journal of Financial Economics*, Vol. 6, pp. 333–64.

Pettit, R. (1972) 'Dividend announcements, security performance and capital market efficiency', *Journal of Finance*, Vol. 27, pp. 993–1007.

Pettit, R. (1977) 'Taxes, transaction cost and clientele effects of dividends', *Journal of Financial Economics*, Vol. 5, December, pp. 419–36.

Porterfield, J. (1965) *Investment Decisions and Capital Costs*, Englewood Cliffs, NJ, Prentice-Hall.

Index